AMSTERDAM

FODOR'S

AMSTERDAM

FODOR'S TRAVEL GUIDES
New York

FODOR'S AMSTERDAM
has been abridged from
FODOR'S HOLLAND 1984

All the following Guides are current (most of them also in
the Hodder and Stoughton British edition).

FODOR'S COUNTRY
AND AREA TITLES:

AUSTRALIA, NEW
ZEALAND AND
SOUTH PACIFIC
AUSTRIA
BELGIUM AND
LUXEMBOURG
BERMUDA
BRAZIL
CANADA
CANADA'S MARITIME
PROVINCES
CARIBBEAN AND
BAHAMAS
CENTRAL AMERICA
EASTERN EUROPE
EGYPT
EUROPE
FRANCE
GERMANY
GREAT BRITAIN
GREECE
HOLLAND
INDIA, NEPAL, AND
SRI LANKA
IRELAND
ISRAEL
ITALY
JAPAN
JORDAN AND HOLY
LAND
KOREA
MEXICO
NORTH AFRICA
PEOPLE'S REPUBLIC
OF CHINA
PORTUGAL
SCANDINAVIA
SCOTLAND

SOUTH AMERICA
SOUTHEAST ASIA
SOVIET UNION
SPAIN
SWITZERLAND
TURKEY
YUGOSLAVIA

CITY GUIDES:
AMSTERDAM
BEIJING,
GUANGZHOU,
SHANGHAI
BOSTON
CHICAGO
DALLAS AND FORT
WORTH
GREATER MIAMI
HONG KONG
HOUSTON
LISBON
LONDON
LOS ANGELES
MADRID
MEXICO CITY AND
ACAPULCO
MUNICH
NEW ORLEANS
NEW YORK CITY
PARIS
ROME
SAN DIEGO
SAN FRANCISCO
STOCKHOLM,
COPENHAGEN,
OSLO, HELSINKI,
AND REYKJAVIK
TOKYO
TORONTO
VIENNA
WASHINGTON, D.C.

FODOR'S BUDGET SERIES:

BUDGET BRITAIN
BUDGET CANADA
BUDGET CARIBBEAN
BUDGET EUROPE
BUDGET FRANCE
BUDGET GERMANY
BUDGET HAWAII
BUDGET ITALY
BUDGET JAPAN
BUDGET LONDON
BUDGET MEXICO
BUDGET
SCANDINAVIA
BUDGET SPAIN
BUDGET TRAVEL IN
AMERICA

USA GUIDES:

ALASKA
CALIFORNIA
CAPE COD
COLORADO
FAR WEST
FLORIDA
HAWAII
NEW ENGLAND
PACIFIC NORTH COAST
PENNSYLVANIA
SOUTH
TEXAS
USA (in one volume)

GOOD TIME TRAVEL GUIDES:

ACAPULCO
MONTREAL
OAHU
SAN FRANCISCO

CONTENTS

EUROPE AND
DON'T MISS

Now you can sail the legendary QE2 to or from Europe—
and fly the other way, free! That means you can begin or
end your European vacation with five unforgettable days
and nights on the last of the great superliners. And get
a free British Airways economy-class ticket between
London and most major U.S. cities.

For only $499 extra per person, you can fly a specially
reserved British Airways Concorde between London and
New York, Miami or Washington, D.C.

Only the QE2 offers four top restaurants and five
lively nightspots. A glittering disco, a glamorous casino
and a 20,000-bottle wine cellar. The famed "Golden
Door Spa at Sea,"® with yoga and aerobic dance, a gym
and jogging deck, saunas, swimming pools and Jacuzzi®
Whirlpool Baths.

- Wide choice of crossings between England and New
  York, some calling on Boston, Philadelphia or Port
  Everglades, as well.
- Cunard's choice European tours—varying in length,
  attractively priced, either escorted or independent—all
  include a QE2 crossing.
- 20 percent discount at Cunard hotels—including
  London's fabulous Ritz—and at Inter-Continental
  Hotels throughout Europe.
- Enchanting QE2 and Vistafjord European cruises,
  which may be combined with a crossing.

For all the facts, including any requirements or
restrictions, contact your travel agent or Cunard, Dept. F84,
P.O. Box 999, Farmingdale, NY 11737; (212) 661-7777.

CUNARD

Certain restrictions apply to free airfare and Concorde programs.
All programs are subject to change. See your travel agent.

THE QE2:
THE MAGIC.

QUEEN
ELIZABETH 2
FOR ONCE IN YOUR LIFE, LIVE.

British Registry

AMSTERDAM

City of a Thousand and One Bridges

Nearly 1,000 years ago, so the legend goes, two fishermen and their dog beached their boat on a sandbank where the river Amstel flowed into the IJ, the old Dutch word for water. They settled there, prospered and were joined by others.

By the 12th century their settlement was still little more than a small fishing village, and not nearly as important as the surrounding towns—Kampen and Zolle to the east, Delft, Dordrecht and Leiden to the south. The village was named after the river and the dam that had afterwards been built there: Amstelledamme.

Despite their insignificance, the people of the village were clearly both shrewd and able. For example, it was only in 1275 that Count Floris V, after many unsuccessful attempts, succeeded in annexing the town to his own lands, and then only after having granted unusual tax

1

exemptions and a lucrative beer-producing monopoly. By 1300 Amstel-ledamme had grown sufficiently to be awarded a city charter.

Its prosperity continued to increase over the next 200 years. But it was the fall of Antwerp, in what is today Belgium, to Spain in 1576 that provided the major spur to the city's growth. Most of Antwerp's merchants moved north to Amsterdam, bringing their wealth and trading connections.

The city embarked on a period of rapid expansion and fast-growing prosperity. Trade was the corner stone of the city's success. Indeed so successful were the city's merchants, that by 1600 their merchant fleet was larger than those of all the rest of the Low Countries' combined. Following the establishment of the East India Company in 1602, the city rose to the peak of its influence and its ships were seen in every corner of the globe. The Bank of Amsterdam, one of the oldest in the world, was established in 1609.

The key to this spectacular mercantile success story was water, or, to be more exact, the canal system, which remains one of the city's most prominent features. The first canals had been built essentially as defensive moats, but by 1600 they came to be used for trading purposes. The building in 1610 of the Herengracht, Keizergracht and Prinsengracht canals in the city center was the first step in turning the city into a vast port. More were gradually added throughout the 17th century, until by the latter part of the century it was possible to unload cargoes in the heart of the city direct from the ships that had carried them there.

By now much of the city had assumed its present day appearance. Many of the houses whose upper stories were used for storing this flood of tea, spices, silks, furs, and whatnot, can still be seen. The heavy beams that jut out from their topmost gables lack only a rope and the men to pull it; the patrician mansions seem still to echo with the steps of the burghers whose portraits were painted by Rembrandt and Frans Hals.

Water was the city's nemesis as well. Twice during the 17th century the locks were opened and the surrounding countryside flooded in defense against the attacks of Prince William II and Louis XIV. In January, 1795, however, the stratagem failed when the temperature fell and the waters froze, thus enabling Napoleon's cavalry to ride across the ice and capture the proud city for France. Even before this time, moreover, the Zuiderzee had begun to silt up. Only ships with flat bottoms and relatively shallow draft could clear the mudbanks, and this during an era when the British were learning to construct stout, deep-keeled vessels that could carry twice the cargo of a Dutch boat twice as fast. Commerce stagnated from the late 17th century until the completion of the North Holland Canal in 1825 and the North Sea

Canal in 1876, while England supplanted Holland as mistress of the seas.

The Spanish also had a hand in making Amsterdam great. Not only did they suppress rival Antwerp but the dreaded Inquisition drove out liberal Catholics, Protestants, and Jews alike, many of whom settled in Holland's leading city where religious toleration and freedom of conscience also attracted certain Separatists or Pilgrims from England, some of whom in 1620 set sail for the Americas where they founded Plymouth, Massachusetts. After the revocation of the Edict of Nantes, these Flemish, Spanish, Portuguese and English refugees were joined by French Protestants. Most of the families who sought asylum in Amsterdam were hard-working, thrifty and skilled in trade or industry. Their talents, their money, and their gratitude to the city that had made them welcome had a catalytic effect on the Dutch themselves.

Today, Amsterdam is a bustling, vigorous city. It is the capital of the Netherlands and with its new suburban agglomeration, has a population of about 690,000. It is the fourth greatest European attraction, after Rome, London and Paris and celebrated its 700th birthday in 1975.

Exploring Amsterdam

By whatever means you arrive in Amsterdam—ship, train, plane, or car—you will necessarily be struck by the symmetrical rings of canals and the 1,100 bridges lacing them together. They are the most characteristic features of this delightful bourgeois city whose character is indelibly stamped with the taste and philosophy of the early 17th century. Time has vindicated its builders, and if few of the stately patrician houses are still owned by merchant princes, few have been allowed to fall into disrepair. Nowhere else in Europe has so brief a moment of history been so faithfully preserved for the delectation, and perhaps the envy, of our ultrasonic age.

A glance at the map confirms the relatively ordered layout of Amsterdam's heart. Imagine a horizontal line with a dip in its middle. The left-hand side of the line is the North Sea Canal, an engineering accomplishment of the first magnitude that cuts a 15-mile swath through what was once sand dunes to provide a direct outlet to the ocean. The right-hand side of the line is the IJ River (pronounced "eye"), which once flowed into the brackish Zuiderzee and thence into the North Sea by a round-about route that led north past Hoorn, Enkhuizen, and Den Oever. Today, of course, the Zuiderzee is a fresh-water lake called the IJsselmeer in honor of this selfsame river. Along both sides of this line is a complex of piers, harbors, drydocks, warehouses, cranes, and other

AMSTERDAM

1. VVV Tourist Information Office
2. Central Station
3. St. Nicolaaskerk
4. Oude Kerk (Old Church)
5. Nieuwe Kerk (New Church)
6. Koninklijk Paleis (Royal Palace)
7. Main Post Office
8. Anne Frank Huis
9. Joordan District
10. Historisch Museum (Historical Museum)
11. Zuiderkerk (South Church)
12. Museum Het Rembrandthuis
    (Rembrandt's House)
13. Zoological Gardens
14. Rijksmuseum
15. Rijksmuseum Vincent Van Gogh
16. Stedelijk Museum (Municipal Museum)
17. Stadsschouwburg (Theater)
C Canal Trips

SCALE
0 ————————— ¼ mile
0 ————————— 400m

Begijnhof – Begijnensteeg (entrance between
18th century court 130 & 132 Kalverstraat) open late
other entrance on Spui

maritime facilities that testify to Amsterdam's importance as a center of world trade.

The dip in the middle of our hypothetical line marks the point at which an artificial island was built to receive the Central Station (1889), whose elaborate towers and cluttered façade were designed by Cuypers in a style that is euphemistically called Dutch Renaissance. The medieval core of Amsterdam, marked by a confusion of waterways that have since been partially filled in (Damrak and Rokin were once canals), is directly below this dip and thus within a few minutes' walk of the station itself. Around this core you'll notice four semicircular rings of canals, with two more at a somewhat greater distance. Planted with elms and lined with gabled, red-brick mansions and storehouses, they are best explored on foot. We seriously advise you to do your exploring with map in hand. The concentrically circular nature of the city's layout makes it terribly easy to start walking in exactly the opposite direction from the one you thought you were going.

A favorite itinerary takes about an hour and follows the east or inner side of the Herengracht from the Raadhuisstraat (behind the Dam and the Royal Palace) to the south and then the east as far as Thorbeckeplein and Reguliersgracht. Americans may wish to detour briefly to the building at Singel 460, today used for auctions, where John Adams obtained the first foreign loan ($2 million) of the infant United States from the banking house of Van Staphorst in 1782. Other loans from this and other houses soon followed to a total of $30 million, a generous Dutch gesture of confidence in the future of America.

Everything within the Lijnbaansgracht or outermost canal is called the Centrum. Everything beyond belongs to the modern development of Amsterdam and is subdivided into West, Zuid (south), and Oost (east). Knife-like, the broad Amstel River pushes its way between Zuid and Oost into the Centrum, where its waters are partitioned into three canals, eventually mingling with the IJ. Visitors may also be interested in Amsterdam's two tunnels, one under the IJ and the other leading to the Zaan area. Perhaps the best introduction to Amsterdam is on one of the frequent canal and city tours. We give full details in the Practical Information section at the end of this chapter.

From the Central Station to the Dam

As you emerge from the Central Station, the Haarlemmerstraat lies just to the right. A tablet at No. 75 (now an orphanage) commemorates the occasion in 1623 when the directors of the Dutch West India Company planned the founding of Nieuw Amsterdam on the southernmost tip of the island of "Manhattes." Two years later the first permanent settlement was made, followed in 1626 by the purchase of a good part of the island from the native Indians "for the value of 60 guilders". In 1664, the colony was seized by the English and renamed New York.

The street directly opposite the station is Prins Hendrikkade, where to the left is Oude (Old) St. Nicolaaskerk. This is one of the oldest parts of the city (the church was consecrated in 1306). It is also the heart of the red light district. The church is notable for its organ, made most famous by the late 16th-century composer Jan Sweelinck. He is buried in the church, as is Rembrandt's wife Saskia. Three stained glass windows, dating from 1555 but extensively restored from 1761–63, and a lovely carillon (complex set of bells) are also worth taking in. During the summer organ concerts are held on Tuesday, Wednesday, Friday and Saturday evening.

Beside St. Nicolaaskerk is the tower of the Schreierstoren (the Criers' Tower or Weeping Tower), where seafarers used to say goodbye to their women before setting off to faraway places. At the angle of Geldersekade and Oudezijdskolk, it was erected in 1487 and a tablet marks the point from which Henry Hudson set sail in the *Half Moon* on April 4, 1609 on a voyage that took him to what is now New York and the river that bears his name. The "Weeping Tower" is now used as a combined reception and exposition center and old-world tavern. It also houses the world's first diamond museum. Farther left (east) at No. 131 is the house of Admiral De Ruyter, who, among other things, sought to avenge the English capture of Nieuw Amsterdam by sailing up the Thames and creating a panic in London in 1667.

More or less behind the Schreirstoren at Oudezijds Voorburgwal 40 is the Amstelkring Museum whose façade carries the inscription "Ons' Lieve Heer Op Solder" or "Our Dear Lord In The Attic." In 1578 Amsterdam embraced Protestantism and, just as reformist sects had previously been forbidden by Catholicism, forbade the Church of Rome. So great was the tolerance of the municipal authorites, however, that clandestine Catholic chapels were allowed to exist as long as their activities were reasonably discreet. At one time, in fact, there were 62 such institutions in Amsterdam alone. The present one, contained in three separate houses built around 1661, was installed in 1663 in the attics of the houses, whose lower floors were ordinary dwellings. It was in use until 1887, the year that the St. Nicolaaskerk opposite the Central Station was consecrated for Catholic worship, since which time it has been preserved by both Protestant and Catholic owners as a monument to toleration in the midst of bigotry. The baroque altar with its revolving tabernacle, the swinging pulpit that can be stowed out of sight, the upstairs gallery, and the display cases in some of the adjoining rooms are all unusually interesting.

Returning to the Damrak, the broad thoroughfare that leads towards the Dam from the Central Station, we pass the piers of excursion boats and reach the Beurs or Exchange, designed by Berlage in a style that, if heavy, is at least free of the excesses of the Dutch Renaissance style of the station and the Rijksmuseum.

If you continue east another three or four blocks, you pass through the red-light district, known as the *walletjes* or *rosse buurt,* where ladies of easy virtue sit behind their picture windows and knit or lacquer their nails while waiting for callers. Small bars around this area are centers of information about the more lurid nightlife possibilities, but some care is needed in accepting advice or offers of guided tours. Just beyond is the Nieuwmarkt or New Market dominated by the five-towered Waag or Weigh House. Like the Schreierstoren, it was orginally part of the town wall, in this case a gate. In 1617 it was turned into a weigh house and guildhouse.

The Dam and the Koninklijk Paleis

Instead of turning aside, however, let's continue up the Damrak to the Dam, the broadest square in the old section of town and the focal point of commercial and touristic activity. To the left you'll note the simple monument to Dutch victims of World War II. The 12 urns contain soil from the 11 provinces and from the former Dutch East Indies, now Indonesia. The old name for this part of the Square is Vischmarkt (Fishmarket) where the boats of the fishing fleet would come in and sell their catch.

The Koninklijk Paleis (Royal Palace) or Dam Palace, a vast, well-proportioned structure completed in 1655, was built originally to replace the city hall that had stood on the same site but had burned down. Remarkably, it is built on 13,659 piles, an excellent illustration of the problems posed by building on the marshy soil of this part of Holland and the extraordinary lengths required to circumvent them. The great pedimental sculptures are an allegorical representation of Amsterdam surrounded by Neptune and mythological sea-creatures. The seven archways at street level symbolize the then seven provinces of the Netherlands, although the entrance, oddly enough, is on the opposite side of the building. In 1808 it was converted into a palace for Louis Bonaparte, Napoleon's brother, who abdicated two years later. Theoretically, it is now the official residence of Queen Beatrix, but she seldom uses it, preferring to live at Huis ten Bosch in Den Haag where she took up residence after becoming Queen in 1980. The Dam Palace now sees only an occasional reception for a visiting Head of State and the Queen's annual New Year reception of the whole diplomatic corps. During the summer the Palace is open to the public.

Directly behind the Palace is the main post office. From here the Raadhuistraat leads west across three canals to the Westermarkt and the Westerkerk, or West Church, built in 1631 by Pieter de Keyser to plans drawn up by his father, Hendrick (who was also responsible for the Zuiderkerk and Noorderkerk). Its 275-ft. tower, the highest in the city, has a large Emperor's crown commemorating Maximilian of Austria at its summit. It also houses an outstanding carillon. Rembrandt and his son Titus are buried here (lying side by side), and Queen Beatrix was married here.

Opposite, at number six Westermarkt, Descartes, the great French 17th-century philosopher *(Cogito, ergo sum)* lived for a brief period in 1634. The house is identified by a commemorative plaque. Another, more famous house, it found further down the same street. This is the Anne Frank Huis, immortalized in the immensely moving diary kept by the young Anne Frank from 1942–44. The Franks, a German-Jewish family, had emigrated to Amsterdam in 1933, following Hitler's rise to power. They managed to evade the Nazis for over two years after the invasion of Holland in May 1940, before moving into the house in July 1942. Here they hid in empty, barren rooms, reached by a small, cleverly-disguised passage leading off the library, and here Anne kept her sad record of two increasingly fraught years before their inevitable capture and deportation to Auschwitz. Her father was the only member of the family to survive. The diary, miraculously, also survived, and was found lying on the floor of the small apartment. A small exhibition on the Holocaust can also be found in the house.

Walking north up the Prinsengracht, you reach the Noordkerk, built in 1623 by de Keyser (see above). In the square in front of the church, the Noorderplein, there is a bird market every Saturday.

From the Dam you can also turn into the Kalverstraat, the single most important shopping street in Amsterdam, which leads south from the left-hand side of the palace. At No. 92 is the beautiful Renaissance (1581) gate of the Burgerweeshuis or City Orphanage, once a monastery, which has an ever older door around the corner to the right in St. Luciensteeg. The inner court dates from about 1670. The black and red coloring in the coat of arms of Amsterdam was reflected in the uniforms of the orphans; they had one red and one black sleeve so they could be identified as belonging to the orphanage.

Continuing down Kalverstraat, turn right into Begijnsteeg, which leads to the delightful Begijnhof, a charming almshouse boasting one of the only two remaining authentic Gothic façades in Amsterdam. Founded in 1346, the houses enclosing the original courtyard date from the 14th to the 17th century. It now adjoins the rehoused Historisch Museum, enlarged and enriched for the 700th anniversary celebrations of the city in 1975. Room after room documents the history of the city with old maps, documents, plans and works of art. Opposite the church, which was given to Amsterdam's English Reformed community more than 300 years ago, is a secret Catholic chapel built in 1671. The Kalverstraat, Heiligeweg and Leidsestraat are all a pedestrian precinct as far as the Dam from the Leidseplein.

Muntplein to Rembrandt's House

The next street to cross Kalverstraat is Spui. A right turn here would bring us to Singel and, following the tram tracks, to Leidsestraat, another important shopping street, which terminates in the Leidseplein with its Municipal Theater and other amusements. On the Singel's west bank, just past the lock by the Open Haven, is what is often erroneously called the narrowest house in Amsterdam. In fact it is just a door giving onto a small alley. The real thing is at number 166 Singel; it's called Den Gulden Fonteyn and houses a gallery.

Continuing straight along Kalverstraat instead, you soon reach the Muntplein with its 1620 Munttoren or Mint Tower, a graceful structure whose clock and bells still seem to mirror the Golden Age. West from the Muntplein is the flower market on Singel canal. Reguliersbreestraat leads east from this point to the Rembrandtsplein and, to the right, Thorbeckeplein, where many cafés and bars are clustered. From the latter square, the Reguliersgracht or canal leads south across the ring canals, crossing them on picturesque bridges.

We turn left (north) out of the Muntplein, however, and cross Rokin, another shopping street, to the bridge that connects with Nieuwe Doelenstraat, which is lined with some of Amsterdam's leading hotels. It in turn merges with Kloveniersburgwal, on whose left-hand side is the University, founded in 1632 and housed in an 18th-century hospital. Today it has over 10,000 students.

We cross the canal ourselves and follow the Raamgracht east to Zwanenburgwal, where the bridge to the left leads across to Jodenbreestraat. At number four is the house where Rembrandt lived from 1639 to 1658, now the Museum Het Rembrandthuis. It was built in 1606, originally with only two stories. Rembrandt bought it when he was at the height of his popularity as Amsterdam's most fashionable portrait painter. The ground floor was used for living quarters, the upper floor was Rembrandt's studio. For some five years, Rembrandt and his wife Saskia lived here in considerable pomp. But following the death of Saskia in 1642, the great man became increasingly introspective and his business gradually declined, though his output remained as prodigious as ever. Finally, in 1658 he was forced to sell the house to meet the demands of a multitude of creditors, and with his mistress Hendrijke Stoffels, who had originally been his housekeeper, and son Titus, moved to the much less prestigious Rozengracht, beyond the Westermarkt. The house was acquired by the city in 1906, and opened as a museum five years later. It is fascinating to visit, both as a general record of life in 17th-century Amsterdam and as a vivid record of the life and working methods of the presiding genius of the 17th century in Holland.

As the name Jodenbreestraat suggests, Rembrandt's house was located in the midst of Amsterdam's Jewish quarter, a circumstance that is reflected in the many Old Testament scenes painted by the master. A block away at Waterlooplein 41, the Portuguese Jew and philosopher Baruch Spinoza was born in 1632. The Dutch Israelite and Portuguese Israelite synagogues were built between 1671 and 1675, a few hundred yards east. The Waterlooplein is also the site of the new Stopera building. The unusual name is derived from its role as Town Hall (Stadhuis) and Opera House. The famous Waterlooplein flea market has now moved to Valkenburgerstraat.

At the northern end of Jodenbreestraat is the Zuiderkerk, the third and final city church on this route designed by Hendrik de Keyser. Built between 1603 and 1611, it was Amsterdam's first post-Reformation church.

Jodenbreestraat continues east under different names to the botanical gardens (Hortus Botanicus), the zoo (Natura Artis Magistra), and the aquarium, which can be reached by following the tramline. Another half mile in the same easterly direction brings you to the Tropenmuseum or Tropical Museum which recently reopened after extensive modification. Its aim is to present the problems of the Third World, and there is a theater (the Soeterijn) where movies and plays from the Third World are to be seen.

Amsterdam's Museum Quarter

On the southernmost edge of the outer Singelgracht canal, a few minutes walk from the Leidseplein, you'll come to one of the cultural centers of Amsterdam. This is the site of three of the most distinguished museums in Holland—the Rijksmuseum, the Stedelijk Museum and the Vincent van Gogh Museum. Of the three, the Rijksmuseum, easily recognized by its cluster of towers, is the most prestigious and important.

It was founded originally by Louis Bonaparte in 1808, but the present rather lavish building dates from 1885. The museum contains significant collections of furniture, textiles, ceramics, sculpture and prints, as well as Italian, Flemish and Spanish paintings, many of the highest quality. But the great pride of the Rijksmuseum is its collection of 16th- and 17th-century Dutch paintings, a collection unmatched by any other in the world.

Perhaps the single most famous painting is Rembrandt's *The Night Watch* (there are several complete rooms on the ground floor devoted exclusively to Rembrandt), commissioned by the Company of Captain Cocq and Lieutenant van Ruytenburg and completed in 1642. The picture was originally even larger than it is today (a spectacular 14 by 12 feet). But in 1711 it was transferred to the War Council in what is today the Royal Palace, and in order to install it in its new location it was necessary to cut 26 inches from the width and 11 from the height. The title of the picture is actually rather misleading. It was long assumed, quite naturally, that Rembrandt's dark and mysterious picture represented a night scene. In fact, it was only when the painting was cleaned in 1947 and layer after layer of ancient varnish painstakingly removed that it became clear that the picture was of a daytime scene. Nonetheless, the original name has continued to be used. The picture also had to be restored in 1975 after it was slashed by a crazed visitor to the museum.

There is more, much more, in the Rijksmuseum: among the more than 3,000 paintings there are jewel-like vignettes by Jan Vermeer, landscapes by Ruysdael and Hobbema, pastorals by Paulus Potter, boisterous domestic scenes by Jan Steen, vigorous portraits by Frans Hals, cool interiors by Pieter de Hoogh, peasant scenes by Van Ostade. Allow at least two hours just to sample these riches, then relax in the pleasant restaurant for a snack, before going on to see the 50-odd galleries containing the magnificent collection of furniture, glass, porcelain, gold and silver. A new wing adds art and artifacts from prehistory to 1900. There is also an Asiatic department in the basement.

A few blocks down the road is the van Gogh Museum, opened in 1972. The largest collection of works by van Gogh in the world, the museum contains 200 paintings and 500 drawings by the artist, as well as 600 of his letters and some 50 works by other painters of the period. The most important paintings are on the second level, while the drawings are displayed on the third.

A stone's throw away is the Stedelijk (Municipal) Museum, housed in a late 19th-century neo-Classical pile, with a new wing added in the '50s. The museum has a magnificent collection of modern art, with all the major figures well represented. It also arranges frequent and usually stimulating exhibitions, often as many as 30 a year.

Diagonally opposite the Stedelijk Museum at the end of the broad Museumplein is the Concertgebouw, the home of Amsterdam's Concertgebouw Orchestra. The building has two auditoriums, the smaller one being used for chamber music and recitals. A block or two away in the opposite direction is Vondelpark, an elongated rectangle of paths, lakes and pleasant shady trees. A monument honors the 17th-century epic poet Vondel, after whom the park is named. From

Wednesday to Sunday in summer free concerts and plays are performed in the park.

While you are exploring Amsterdam, keep one ear cocked for the unmistakable strains of a street organ. Pushed from street corner to street corner by a team of husky men, these remarkable instruments pour forth a torrent of sound generated by a bizarre mixture of drums, pipes, cymbals, and the like. The organ grinder and his mates circulate with jangling cups in which you are urged to drop an appreciative *dubbeltje* or *kwartje*. The virtuosity of selections—jazz, waltzes, round dances, and martial airs—together with the frescoed façade behind whose carved panels the muses labor so mightily, seem somehow symbolic of this proud city that has become strong through diversity and great through zestful enterprise.

One old part of Amsterdam that must be mentioned and is certainly worth exploring is the Jordaan, the area between Rozengracht and Haarlemmerdijk. The canals and side streets in this part all have the names of flowers and plants. Indeed at one time, when this was the French quarter of the city, the area was known as *le jardin,* a name that over the years has become Jordaan. The best time to explore the old town is on a Sunday morning when there are not too many cars and people about.

The Outskirts of Amsterdam

About a mile south of the city is the Olympic stadium, completed for the Olympic Games in 1928 and accommodating 80,000 spectators. Today the stadium is the home of Ajax, one of the country's leading soccer teams. Close by is the Haarlemeer Station, site of the Electricische Museumtramlijn (City Tram Museum). This is one of the very best spots in town for children. Take a ride on one of the old trams (weekends only) to the Amsterdam woods, where, incidentally, a short walk takes you to the delightful old farm house of Meerzicht. Try one of their delicious pancakes!

Just beyond the stadium is one of Amsterdam's proudest achievements: the Bosplan or Forest Park, stretching for several miles, almost to Schiphol Airport. As large as Paris' Bois de Boulogne, twice as big as New York's Central Park, it was started in 1934 as a relief project during the depression. Its more than 2,200 acres is about half woodland and includes mile after mile of bicycle paths, bridle paths, footpaths, and roadways plus an open-air theater, a score of soccer fields, a rowing course 733 meters (2,400 yards) long, and many other sports facilities. The land used for this far-reaching development has been reclaimed at the cost of constructing a 322 kilometer (200-mile) network of drainage pipes. In the past four decades the park has been colonized by birds and other wildlife.

Nearer to Schiphol Airport, Europe's largest artificial ski slope was opened in late 1978. Called the Meerberg, it's near the Sheraton Schiphol Inn, Hoofddorp.

A visit to the new Amstelpark with its modern sculptures, restaurant, sauna and rose exhibition, is a pleasant way to spend an afternoon. The park is close to the RAI fairground.

Despite some complaints that the city is overpriced, overcrowded and over-rated, Amsterdam remains one of Europe's most charming towns. The Dutch take care to preserve their architecture as well as carrying out innovative expansion schemes stretching out into the surrounding countryside. Some fine examples of continental city-planning and urbanization are to be seen, especially towards the Schiphol area, all of them characterized by the Dutch love of greenery, flowers, parks and decorative waters. There is actually an underground metro whose construction was no small job in sandy soil below sea level.

Call in at the VVV in front of Central Station to get particulars of the half-day trips around Amsterdam and make theater reservations. If you feel a little adventurous, ask for the holiday-time plan by which you see Amsterdam on bicycles. The excursion starts around 10, and you collect your tour certificate at 3.15 P.M. with a Dutch drink at a local tavern.

PRACTICAL INFORMATION FOR AMSTERDAM

GETTING TO TOWN FROM THE AIRPORT. Transport from Schiphol Airport (the only airport in the world below sea level, though only by 13 feet) to the city is generally good. KLM (Royal Dutch Airlines) runs a rapid and regular bus service to the Central Station—fare is Fl. 6.50 per person —and there is also a good train/tram service to the Central Station—fare is Fl. 6.30 per person. There is also a regular city bus service, again to the Central Station, every 30 minutes—fare is Fl. 4 per person. All three services also operate to Schiphol from the Central Station.

Taxis, readily available, are expensive, costing from around Fl. 35.

TELEPHONE CODES. The telephone code for Amsterdam is 020. To call any number in this chapter, unless otherwise specified, this prefix must be used. Within the city, no prefix is required.

HOTELS. Most hotels in Amsterdam are inside the concentric ring of canals that surround the downtown area. At Easter and in the peak summer months (mid-June to September) they fill to bursting and advance reservations are essential. The VVV accommodations office in the Central Station can usually find a room for you, however, if you arrive without a booking. (Out of season they can usually also recommend hotels offering discounts). Few downtown hotels have parking facilities.

We have divided the hotels in our listings into four categories—Deluxe, Expensive, Moderate and Inexpensive. In *Deluxe* hotels, two people in a double room can expect to pay from Fl. 210 to Fl. 450, in *Expensive* hotels from Fl. 160 to Fl. 310, in *Moderate* hotels from Fl. 75 to Fl. 220 and in *Inexpensive* hotels from Fl. 60 to Fl. 100. Most hotels, particularly at the upper end of the scale, have rooms in more than one price category and a consequently wide range of prices. Be very sure to check *before* making your reservations what category of room you are booking. All prices include 15% service charge, tax and, usually, breakfast (again, check if this is included). Deluxe and Expensive hotels all have bathrooms in the rooms; in the lower grades bathrooms are usually down the corridor, but they will always be spotlessly clean.

Prices for single rooms are around 65 to 75% of double room costs.

Deluxe

Amstel. 1 Prof. Tupplein; 226060. 118 rooms with bath. Situated on the Amstel River, it has a reputation for solid comfort—and for being the most expensive hotel in the city. Room standard varies a bit. The terrace is delightful in summer.

Amsterdam Hilton. 138 Apollolaan; 780780. 276 rooms with bath. Glassed-in floral garden, heated in winter. Boasts the *Diamond* restaurant and *Half Moon Bar.* KLM buses to/from airport stop here.

Apollo. 2 Apollolaan (main entrance on Stadionweg); 735922. At the junction of five canals, has 225 rooms each with bath. There is a fine restaurant, private landing stage and a large car park. (Do not confuse this with a less pretentious Apollo close by.)

De L'Europe. 2 Nieuwe Doelenstraat; 234836. Opposite the Muntplein with a view of the Amstel. 80 rooms with bath; more comfortable than its Victorian facade suggests. Excellent restaurant for dinner and *Le Relais* for grills.

Marriott. 19–21 Stadhouderskade; 835151. 400 rooms; excellent dining in the popular *Port O'Amsterdam* restaurant. Several deluxe suites. Right in the city center.

Okura Intercontinental. 175 Ferd. Bolstraat; 787111. 402 rooms with bath, 20 suites, studios and Japanese-style rooms. Several restaurants including the fine *Ciel Bleu,* serving the best Japanese food in Holland.

Schiphol Hilton. At the airport; 020–5115911. 204 rooms, all with bath; 24-hour room service, ideal for inter-flight business meetings. Indoor pool.

Sonesta. 1 Kattengat; 212223. 425 rooms, all with bath. Well-designed modern hotel with every comfort. *Rib Room* restaurant, *de Serre* and *Koepel* cafés give full range of eating possibilities. Attached to the Sonesta complex are several old houses and a restored Lutheran church, a huge rotunda used for conferences and regular concerts. One of the most intriguing hotel concepts in Europe.

Expensive

Alexander. 444 Prinsengracht; 267721. 25 rooms with bath. Is located above (and belongs to) the *Dikker en Thijs* restaurant.

American. 97 Leidsekade; 245322. 185 rooms with bath. Next door to the City Theater, a few minutes from the town center.

Arthur Frommer. 46 Noorderstraat; 220328. 90 rooms. Dinner only in restaurant.

Caransa. 19 Rembrandtsplein; 229455. 70 rooms with bath; restaurant.

Crest Hotel. 2 de Boelelann; 429855. 263 rooms with bath or shower, penthouse suites. *Bourgogne* restaurant, coffee shop, bar.

Dikker en Thijs Garden. 7 Dijsselhofplantsoen. 98 rooms. Close to KLM shuttle bus stop; has *de Kersentuin* restaurant.

Doelen. 24 Nieuwe Doelenstraat; 220722. 86 rooms, most with bath. Traditional, old-fashioned comfort. Ask for a room on the quieter canal-side. Excellent restaurant and bar.

Hotel Ibis. 181 Schipholweg; 02968–1234. 400 rooms, and located in Badhoevedorp, near the airport (has shuttle service). Restaurants, 24-hour coffee shop, bar.

Krasnapolsky. 9 Dam; 549111. 255 rooms, most with bath.

Memphis. 87 De Lairessestraat; 733141. 90 rooms with bath or shower, furnished in French style. Good restaurant.

Novotel. 10 Europaboulevard; 442851. With 600 rooms and several restaurants, this is Holland's largest hotel. Modern and a little anonymous.

Parkhotel. 25 Stadhouderskade; 717474. 183 rooms, most with bath. A step away from the Rijksmuseum and next door to the Vondelpark.

Pulitzer. 323 Prinsengracht; 228333. In a row of restored 17th-century houses. 190 rooms, each with bath. Restaurant, bar. A Golden Tulip hotel.

Sheraton Schiphol Inn. 495 Kruisweg, Hoofddorp; 02503–15851. No charge for youngsters sharing adults' room. Pets are welcome.

Victoria. 1–5 Damrak, opposite the station; 234255. 150 rooms, most with bath.

Moderate

Ambassade. 341 Herengracht; 262333. 27 rooms, all with bath. Beautiful canal-side location. Good value.

Amster Center. 255 Herengrach; 221727. 110 rooms with bath.

Asterix. 14 Den Texstraat; 262396. 35 rooms, some with bath. Very good value. Closed Jan. and Feb.

Beethoven. 43 Beethovenstraat; 723900. 52 rooms, half with bath or shower.

Carlton. 18 Vijzelstraat; 222266. Central but noisy. 150 rooms with bath.

Casa 400. 75 James Wattstraat; 651171. 400 rooms with shower. All the amenities—American bar, two restaurants, sun lounges, plus a nursery for the kids. Closed Jan.–May.

Centraal. 7 Stadhouderskade; 185765. Near Vondelpark and Leidseplein, ten minutes from downtown. 119 rooms with bath. A Golden Tulip hotel.

De Roode Leeuw. 93 Damrak; 240396. 80 rooms, over half with bath. Pleasant sidewalk terrace. Central.

Delphi. 101 Apollolaan; 795152. 48 rooms with bath. Friendly atmosphere.

Estherea. 305 Singel; 245146. 70 rooms.

Euromotel Schiphol. 20 Oude Haagseweg (tel. 179005). On the main road to Den Haag. 150 rooms with shower.

Euromotel E9. Sloterweg; 658181. On the highway to Utrecht. 140 rooms with shower.

Fantasia. 16 Nieuwe Keizersgracht; 238259. 20 rooms, a few with bath. At the lower end of the price scale. Closed Jan. and Feb.

Mikado. 107 Amstel; 237068. 25 rooms, most with bath. Reasonable.

Museum. 2–10 P.C. Hoofstraat; 733918. 150 rooms, only a few with bath.

Poort van Cleeve. 178 N.Z.-Voorburgwal; 244860. 110 rooms with bath. Though very central, it breathes antiquity and quietness. Top of this price range.

Sander. 69 Jac. Obrechtstraat. Family atmosphere, excellent service, modest prices.

Schiller. 26 Rembrandtplein; 231660. 86 rooms with bath. Very central. Has popular sidewalk café and restaurant.

Slotania. 133 Slotermeerlaan; 134568. A bit far from the center, but good connections on city transport. Reasonable prices.

Trianon. 3 J.W. Brouwerstraat; 733918. 15 rooms. Located next to the concert hall, the Rijksmuseum and the van Gogh Museum.

Inexpensive

Cok Budget Hotel. 30 Koninginneweg, with an annex next door at 1 Koninglaan; 728095. Simple and comfortable.

Hans Brinker Hotel. 136 Kerkstraat; 220687. 52 rooms, no facilities, but extremely inexpensive.

Paap. 39 Keizersgracht; 249600. 20 rooms, some with bath. Closed Jan.–mid-Mar.

Studenthotel h'88. 88'Herengracht; 244446. Rock-bottom prices (around Fl. 15 including breakfast), in dormitories with minimal comfort; only for the young or brave.

Weichmann. 328 Prinsengracht; 263321. 35 rooms, some with bath.

Youth Hostels. There are a number of youth hostels in Amsterdam offering accommodations for around Fl. 15 per night, including breakfast. Full details are available from Stichting Nederlandse Jeugdherberg Centrale, 4 Prof. Tupplein, Amsterdam; or from the VVV at the Central Station.

Camping. There is a large camp site at 45 Ijsbaanpad (tel. 720916). It is open from April to October but can get very full in high season, so book ahead.

 GETTING AROUND. By Bus, Tram and Metro. Armed with a route map, available from the VVV, you should have no trouble getting around. A zonal fare system is used, with metro tickets purchased from automatic dispensers, tram and bus tickets from drivers (all of whom speak English!). The best bet, however, is to buy a *stripenkaart* (strip ticket) which is good for several journeys or, best of all, an unlimited travel ticket (ask at the VVV for details). These are valid for 1, 2 or 3 days and cost Fl. 6.50, 8.50 and 10.75 respectively.

By Taxi. Taxis are expensive. Flag fall varies from Fl. 2 to Fl. 4, and charges thereafter are Fl. 2 to Fl. 4 per kilometer. Taxis are not usually hailed in the street, but taken from ranks, normally near stations, or at key road intersections. To call a taxi, dial 777777.

On Foot/By Bicycle. Amsterdam is a small congested city full of narrow streets—ideal for exploring on foot. But be sure to get a good map, available from the VVV. Bicycles are available for hire for around Fl. 1.6 per day. They are perhaps the easiest way to get around, but be careful of the traffic. Details, again, available from the VVV.

Canal and City Tours. Perhaps the best and most enjoyable introduction to Amsterdam is a boat trip along the canals. Several operators run trips, usually in glass-roofed boats (particularly important in bad weather). There are frequent departures from starting points opposite the Central Station, beside the Damrack, along the Rokin and Stadhouderskade (near the Rijksmuseum) and from several other spots. Most trips have multilingual guides (a good guide can make all the difference, so make sure you take one of the English-language trips) and last from 1 to 1½ hours. They cost from Fl. 7.50 to Fl. 10. Most also take in the busy harbor. A number have facilities for wheelchairs.

Even more delightful are the night-time trips that run in the summer. They are more expensive (Fl. 27.50 to Fl. 30.50) but wine and cheese are usually included in the price, and in any case the sight of the city's graceful and dignified 17th-century mansions slipping by in the twilight, their lights glistening in the water, should not be missed.

But tours around the city are also available and provide a reasonable introduction to Amsterdam. Price is from Fl. 27.50, duration around 3 hours. Most of these trips include a brief visit to the Rijksmuseum (though there's not much you can do there in half an hour) and a visit to a diamond-cutting factory. Tours on Sundays also include a canal trip.

Details of all these excursions are available from the VVV in the Central Station.

TOURIST INFORMATION. The main tourist information office (VVV) is at the Central Station (tel. 020–266444). It is open every day in summer from 8.45 A.M. to 11 P.M.; in winter for shorter periods. The office has an accommodations service for those who arrive without reservations; a small fee is charged for this. They can also make theater and excursion bookings (including canal trips) as well as supplying maps, restaurant lists, sight seeing checklists etc. There is always at least one person on duty who speaks English.

USEFUL ADDRESSES. Travel Agents. *American Express,* 66 Damrak (tel. 62042). *Wagons-Lits/Cooks,* 19 Dam (tel. 65511), and at Amstel Hotel, 1 Prof. Tupplein (tel. 226060). *Lissone-Lindeman,* 91 Damrak (tel. 62448), and 10 Dam (tel. 230951). *Havas-Exprinter,* 106 Leidsestraat (tel. 246949).

Consulates. *American Consulate,* 19 Museumplain (tel. 790321). *British Consulate,* 7Joh. Vermeerstraat (tel. 764343).

Car-Hire. *Avis-Rent-a-Car,* 485 Keizersgracht (tel. 262201). *Hertz,* 333 Overtoom (tel. 122441). *Europcar,* 51–53 Overtoom (tel. 184595).

All the leading car-hire companies have desks at Schiphol Airport.

MUSEUMS. Amsterdam has nearly 50 museums—nearly all of them attractively and imaginatively laid out—ranging from the quaint and local to the internationally renowned. A visit to one or more is largely essential. For the really serious museums goer the Museum Ticket is an excellent buy. That will get you into 16 museums in Amsterdam (and dozens more around the country). Issued by VVV offices, it costs Fl. 1.05 for those under 25 and Fl. 50 for those 25 and over. Note that most museums close on Mondays.

Allard Pierson Museum. Oude Turfmarkt. Archeological finds from Mesopotamia, Egypt, Greece, Italy. Open 10–5, Tues.–Sat., 1–5 Sun. Closed Mon. Adm. Fl. 1.2.

Anne Frank Huis (Anne Frank Museum). 263 Prinsengracht. The house in which the young Jewish girl Anne Frank, author of the famous diary, hid from the Nazis during World War II. The rooms where the family was hidden are open to visitors and there are other moving wartime exhibits. Open 10–5, Tues.–Sat., 1–5 Sun. Closed Mon. Adm. Fl. 3.

Amsterdams Historisch Museum (Historical Museum). 92 Kalverstraat. Housed in a renovated orphanage. Good depiction of the city from earliest times. Interesting coffee and diamond trade exhibits; fascinating collection of jewelry. Fairly good restaurant. Open 10–5, Tues.–Sat., 1–5 Sun. Closed Mon. Adm. Fl. 3.50.

Aviodome Nationaal Lucht- en Ruimtevaartmuweum (Aviodome National Aeronautical Museum). Schiphol. Exhibition of aviation and space travel, past and present, with a glimpse into the future. Open 1 Apr.–31 Oct. daily 10–5; Nov.–31 March, Tues.–Sun. 10–5. Adm. Fl. 4.50.

Begijnhof. Entrance on Spui. A kind of openair museum with a church and nuns' living quarters dating back to 1346.

Bijbels Museum. 366 Herengracht. Biblical antiquities from Palestine, Egypt and Mesopotamia. Open 10–5, Tues.–Sat., 1–5 Sun. Closed Mon. Adm. Fl. 1.2.

Collectie Six. 218 Amstel. Home of the descendants of Jan Six; you can visit it by obtaining an introduction card from the Rijksmuseum. Ten generations ago Jan Six was, among other things, a patron and friend of Rembrandt, who painted his portrait, which still hangs here. For opening times, check when you obtain the card.

Electrische Museumtramlijn Amsterdam (Amsterdam Tram Museum). In the old Haarlemmermeer Station. Includes rides on the old city trams.

Filmmuseum Nederlands. 3 Vondelpark. Film reviews, photographs, playbills, shows; library; changing exhibitions. Open Tues.–Thurs. 10–12.30 and 1.30–5. Closed holidays. Adm. Fl. 1.

Fodor Museum. 609 Keizersgracht. Works by young modern artists which are also for sale. (No connection with the publishers of this Guide!) Open 10–5, Tues.–Sat., 1–5 Sun. Closed Mon. Adm. 50 cents.

Madame Tussaud, Kalverstraat 156. Tells the story of Dutch people and events through the ages in life-size wax models. Open daily from 10–6, in summer 10–7. Adm. Fl. 5.75.

Museum Amstelkring Ons' Lieve Heer op Solder (Our Lord in the Attic). Oudezijds Voorburgwal 40. From the outside this is a typical 17th-century merchants' home. Inside on the top floor, however, is a remarkable attic Catholic church that dates from the Reformation when non-Protestants were forbidden to worship. Every room is a delight. Open Mon.–Fri., 10–5, Sun. 1–5. Adm. Fl. 2. Adm. Fl. 2.

Museum of Architecture. 1a Droogbak. Architecture in Holland and abroad. Open Mon.–Fri. 10–5. Closed public holidays. Adm. free.

Museum Het Rembrandthuis (Rembrandt Museum). Jodenbreestraat 4. Dating from 1606 this fascinating house was the home of the painter from 1639–1658. Open Mon.–Fri. 10–5, Sun. and holidays 1–4.

Nederlands Scheepvaart Museum (Maritime Museum). 1 Kattenburgerplein. Historical ship models, paintings, prints, maps, nautical instruments. Open 10–5, Tues.–Sat., 1–5 Sun. Closed Mon. Adm. Fl. 4.50.

NINT, Nederlands Instituut voor Nijverheid en Techniek (Dutch Institute for Industry and Technology). Tollstr. Exhibitions relating to natural science and technology. Open Mon.–Fri. 10–4, Sat. 1–5 (1 Oct.–30 Apr. also Sun. 1–5) Closed public holidays. Adm. Fl. 3.

Rijksmuseum. 42 Stadhouderskade. A vast Victorian red-brick building facing the outermost of the city's concentric ring of canals and the country's most prestigious and important museum. Superb collection of Dutch 16th- and 17th-century paintings, plus magnificent Flemish, Italian and Spanish works. Other departments include Asiatic and graphic art, a print room with ancient and modern drawings, a library containing 35,000 books on art, and Dutch sculpture and decorative art up to the 19th-century. Well over 30 galleries of 18th-century furniture, glass, porcelain, gold and silver, make it the largest collection of its kind in Europe. Useful cafeteria available. Conducted tours at 11 and 2.30. Open 10–5, Tues–Sat., 1–5 Sun. Closed Mon. Adm. Fl. 4.50

Rijksmuseum Vincent van Gogh. Next door to the Stedelijk Museum. Unrivaled collection of 200 paintings, 400 drawings and 600 letters by the artist, along with library and many other documents and paintings. Attractive cafeteria with terrace in summer. Open 10–5, Tues.–Sat., 1–5 Sun. Closed Mon. Adm. Fl. 4.50.

Stedelijk Museum (Municipal Museum). 13 Paulus Potterstraat. Excellent collections of modern art, plus good late 19th- and early 20th-century works. Open 10–5, Tues.–Sat., 1–5 Sun. Closed Mon.

Theatermuseum. 168 Herengracht. Documents history of the Dutch theater through prints, drawings, costumes, programs etc. Changing exhibitions. Open 10–5, Mon.–Fri., 11–5 Sat., Sun. and public holidays. Adm. Fl. 1.2.

Tropenmuseum (Tropical Museum). 2 Linnaeusstraat. Exhibits on all aspects of the Third World. Open 10–5, Mon.–Fri., 12–5 Sat. and Sun. Adm. Fl. 3.

Waag or St. Anthoniespoort (Weigh House). Nieuwmarkt. Houses Jewish history museum. Open 10–5, Tues.–Sat, 1–5 Sun. Closed Mon.

Willet Holthuysen Museum, 605 Herengracht. Characteristic and delightful 17th-century merchant's mansion. Open 10–5, Tues.–Sat, 1–5 Sun. Closed Mon. Adm. Fl. 2.

BOTANICAL GARDENS, ZOO, AND AQUARIUM. These three make up a large complex just to the east of the downtown area along the Plantage Kerklaan; it's well worth a visit particularly as a change from serious museum visiting. Coming from the downtown area, you first reach the *Hortus Botanicus* (Botanical Gardens), with hothouses and nurseries and plants galore. A block further along is the *Natura Artis Magistra* (better known as the Zoo), an excellent example of its type with everything from insects to elephants. Finally, there is the Aquarium, a characteristic representative of the species; one of the highlights here is the electric eels who are periodically stimulated into lighting up a row of bulbs.

ENTERTAINMENT. Music and Concerts. In the music department, Amsterdam's famous Concertgebouw Orchestra ranks among the foremost in Europe. It plays in the Concertgebouw, Van Baerlestraat 98. Tickets for its performances are so much in demand that people are seated on stage left and right of the orchestra as well as in front. The same building has a smaller auditorium that is used for chamber music, recitals and even jam sessions. As for Opera, the Stadsschouwburg, Leidseplein, is the home of the Netherlands Opera. It is also used for ballets and plays, which are normally presented in Dutch, though during the Holland Festival foreign companies also perform. For information on the Holland Festival contact—Holland Festival, Willemsparkweg 52, 1071 HJ Amsterdam.

For details of current performances—including rock and jazz—see *Amsterdam This Week,* a weekly listing of events and entertainments available free from the VVV. The VVV can also make bookings for most performances.

Movie theaters are scattered throughout Amsterdam, the biggest concentrations being on Leidseplein and Reguliersbreestraat. Performances begin at fixed hours, often 1.30, 3.45, 6.45 and 9.30 P.M. Smoking is forbidden in all theaters and movie houses. Sound tracks are usually in the original language with Dutch subtitles. To see what's playing when and where, see *Amsterdam This Week.*

 ALTERNATIVE AMSTERDAM. Paradiso, still famous from the drug days of the '60s and the provo's (kabouters), is at 6–8 Weteringschans (tel. 64521). Now has pop concerts, classical music, cinema, workshops, jazz, reading table, café, macrobiotic restaurant, etc., as well as being the Punk center of Amsterdam. Open Tues.–Sat., 8–1 A.M., Fri., Sat. 8–2 A.M.

Akhnaton, 25 N.Z., Kolk, a youth center for young working people as well as students. More long-term programs than the first three mentioned, including performances of theater, concerts, films.

Kosmos, 142 Prins Hendrikkade. Meditation center including yoga, zen, astrology, alternative medicine, herbs, food, film, theater, lectures, café, macrobiotic restaurant and even a sauna.

Melkweg (Milky Way), 234a Lijnbaansgracht, behind the main city theater. A multi-media center with film, theater, video, pop, jazz, poetry, mime, jam sessions, tea rooms with a sweet heady scent in the air, art market, etc.

 SHOPPING. Amsterdam's chief shopping streets, which have largely been turned into pedestrian-only areas, are the dignified Leidsestraat; the brighter Kalverstraat; de Nieuwendijk, on the other side of the Dam Square; the Rokin, somber and sedate, where the best antique dealers choose to stand; de Reguliersdwarsstraat, starting at the Muntplein; the Nieuwe Spiegelstraat where a series of old curiosity shops cluster together; the P. C. Hooftstraat strewn with small attractive boutiques favored more by the resident than the tourist; and the Beethovenstraat, which converges with the Stadionweg, where the smart residential south lives and buys.

Markets

There's a lively flea market near the Waterlooplein on Valkenburgerstraat (weekdays only, 10–4). The flower market is held on the Singel during weekdays; a colorful and vivid experience. Noisier, is the bird market held every Wed. and Sat. afternoon in the Noordmarkt. The more studious might be interested in the stamp market, also Wed. and Sat. afternoon, at Nieuwwezijds Voorburgwal and the book market at Oudemanhuispoort, held most days Mon.–Sat.

Diamonds

Moving upmarket rather sharply, no visit to Amsterdam is complete without a visit to one of the major cutting houses. Apart from the fascination of watching the cutting, there is usually no pressure to buy (though male visitors should be careful to keep their womenfolk on a short leash and not let them talk into splashing out—diamonds may be forever, but they are also very expensive!).

Among the leading cutting houses are:

Amsterdam Diamond Center B.V., 1 Rokin; *Coster Diamonds,* 2–4 Paulus Potterstraat; *Gassan Diamond House,* 17–23 Nieuwe Achtergracht; *Holshuysen - Stoeltie B.V.,* 13–17 Wagenstraat; *A. Van Moppes & Zoon B.V.,* 2–6 Albert Cuypstraat.

Most are open from 9–5, and all will be glad to show you around.

Antiques

Amsterdam is one of Europe's leading centers for antiques, from every source, of every type, from every age. The area around Nieuwe Spiegelstraat is full of small antique shops, specialized and general. The Joorden district also has many shops. In addition, there are several important antique markets held each week, featuring stalls for everything from the worthless to the, perhaps, priceless. As well as the flea market on Valkenburgerstraat, other antique markets include: Looiersgracht, at 30 Looiersgracht; de Looier, 187, Lijnbaansgracht, open Thurs., Fri. and Sat.; and Icon, 16 Frederiksplein, Tues. to Sat. Most are open, on days indicated, from 9 to 5.

Porcelain

De Porceleyne Fles, Muntplein 12, offers a fine choice of Royal Delftware, also Meeuw's famous modern pewter in ostrich-necked jugs, plump bowls, straw-handled tea and coffee services. Fine porcelain, particularly imported Wedgwood, is obtainable at *Van Gelder & Co.,* J. Rebelstraat (closed Saturdays), or in their narrow branch store at Van Baerlestraat 40.

Books

Book shops have a very large selection of new editions, second-hand books and even collectors' items in many languages, and so are often worth browsing in for half an hour or so. Bargains can also often be picked up during a stroll through Oudemanhuispoort, a unique market, between Kloveniersburgwal and Oudezijds Burgwal. Don't be put off by these tongue-twisting names; they're easier to get to than pronounce. The *Atheneum Bookshop,* 14-16 Spui, is one of the most wide-ranging and pleasant to browse around. *Allard de Lange,* 62 Damrak, opposite the Bijenkorf, has a fascinating range of maps and travel guides. *De Ronde Regenboog,* van Egenstraat, is good for books covering current issues and critical literature. *De Sleghte,* Kalverstraat (also Coolsingel, Rotterdam) is a good place to browse. They sell foreign books as well as Dutch ones and on any topic you can think of. In addition to that they sell their own reprints of old Dutch maps, engravings and prints at reasonable prices. Also reproductions.

Miscellaneous

Go to *Jacob Hooy* at 12 Kloveniersburgwal, an old-style delicatessen filled with herb pots and drawers of spices in which the firm has been dealing for well over two centuries. You will learn a lot about oriental and exotic flavorings there. If, however, it is cheese you are after, make for *De Fransekaasmaker* at 192 Marnixstraat. They sell 65 different varieties of cheese from many lands.

Most shops have a wide range of French and other foreign clothes, while Dutch ready-to-wear fashions are good quality though more expensive than fashions in Britain or the States. For the young and trendy there are many small boutiques, including some interesting second-hand clothes-shops in the Joordan area.

Lazy (or tired) shoppers could do worse than call in at one of the big department stores like the *Bijenkorf*, Damrak, corner Dam Square, where almost everything is obtainable under one roof. Although not quite so large as Macy's in the US or Selfridges in England, it's got just about everything, including a restaurant where the pancakes are quite delicious. Also *Vroom & Dreesmann*, Kalverstraat near Munt Square, *Hema* (an equivalent of British Woolworth) and *Maison de Bonneterie*, Reguliersdwarsstraat, though the range of articles for sale is rather limited.

Two places of interest near the Sonesta Hotel are—*Holland Happening*, a half-hour audio visual show, and the *Holland Art and Craft Center*, where Dutch craftsmen show their skills and invite participation.

 RESTAURANTS. Amsterdam has an abundance of excellent restaurants in all price categories offering a wide range of international cuisines. Dutch cuisine is naturally the most common (our Dutch *Food and Drink* chapter will introduce you to many of the traditional Dutch specialties you can enjoy here—in typical, unhurried Dutch style, of course) but the city is also famed for its Indonesian restaurants, a legacy of the country's colonial past.

Also recommended for a sample of genuine local life and food are the "brown cafes," so called as they are seldom decorated! They are a cross between a British pub and a French cafe and, apart from the normally exuberant atmosphere, serve good inexpensive food. As well as the many Indonesian restaurants, you might also try Chinese food, usually inexpensive and reliable. Amsterdam, in common with the rest of Europe these days, has its fair share of fast-food hamburger joints—all the familiar names are here—which, though hardly characteristic, are inexpensive and good value. Much more characteristic are the city's traditional herring carts; these can be found in many locations throughout the city.

Best value of all is the Tourist Menu. Over 600 hundred restaurants in Holland serve it (look for the sign outside) and the price is always Fl. 16.25, fully inclusive, for three courses. For those on a tighter budget it is excellent value.

Our restaurant lists are divided into three categories: Expensive, Moderate and Inexpensive. Per person and excluding drinks, you can expect to pay from Fl. 60 in an *Expensive* restaurant, from Fl. 30 to Fl. 50 in a *Moderate* restaurant and from Fl. 25 in an *Inexpensive* restaurant. However, these prices can be no more than approximations of the total cost as most restaurants serve dishes in more than one price category. Similarly, what you drink will affect your bill significantly. So be sure to check the menus posted outside (by law) *before* you go in.

Note also that for more expensive restaurants you should book ahead. Similarly, remember that the Dutch eat early and that many restaurants are accordingly closed as early as 10 P.M. Credit cards are not universally accepted, even in Expensive restaurants, so take cash along for emergencies.

Expensive

Bali. 95 Leidsestraat; 227878. Fast for a day before you come here or you won't be able to finish half the delicious Oriental delicacies you'll be served.

Dikker en Thijs. 438 Prinsengracht; 267721. Elegant restaurant serving fine French cuisine; certainly one of Amsterdam's best. The **Café de Centre,** ground floor, for inexpensive lunches and self-service dinner.

Excelsior. 2 Nieuwe Doelenstraat; 234836. A close rival of Dikker en Thijs for flawless French cooking and elegant atmosphere. Located in the Hotel de l'Europe, sharing its view of the Amstel river.

Ile de France Rôtisserie. 9 Platmanweg, in Amstelveen (a suburb of Amsterdam); 453509. Another quality French restaurant with impeccable food and service.

De Kater. 2–4 Gerard Douplein; 722424. The chef discusses the evening's French specialties with each party. Reservation essential.

Kyo, 2a Jan Luykenstraat; 716916. Known as a mecca for Japanese food. Reservations advisable. Closed Sun.

Prinsenkelder. 438 Prinsengracht. Rather formal, but excellent food, if a little expensive. Closed Sun.

De Silveren Speigel. 4 Kattengat; 246589. Excellent food, but a bit pricey.

t' Swarte Schaep (The Black Sheep). 24 Korte Leidsedwarsstraat; 223021. Dates from 1687, and has one of the largest wine cellars in all of Europe. Cooking is reasonably good, but prices are on the high scale.

Tout Court. 17 Runstraat; 258637. Run by a member of the renowned Fagel family, famed for its French culinary feats. Good for after-theater parties. Closed Mon.

d'Viff Vlieghen (Five Flies). 294 Spuistraat; 248369. Five ancient houses contain a warren of dining rooms, any of which would grace a museum. Menu includes Dutch specialties; game in season. Unfortunately now somewhat touristy.

Yamazato Oriental Restaurant. 175 Ferd. Bolstraat; 787111. Part of Okura Hotel, this is perhaps the best Japanese restaurant in town. Also in the hotel is the popular *Teppan-Yaki.*

Moderate

Adrian. 21 Reguliersdwarsstraat. French cuisine, good wines.

Bodega Keijzer. 96 van Baerlestraat, next to the Concertgebouw, the City Concert Hall; 711441. Very good food, warm atmosphere.

De Boerderij. 69 Korte Leidsedwarsstraat; 236929. *The* place for superb grills, good wines, and cheerful surroundings. Closed Sun.

Café Pacifico. 31 Warmoestraat. Popular, serving Mexican dishes.

Dorrius. 336 Nieuwe Zijds Voorburgwal; 235875. A popular businessmen's haunt serving Dutch specialties. Closed Sun.

Fong Lie. 80 P.C. Hoofstraat; 716404. Chinese food for the knowledgeable. Booking essential. Closed Mon.

Granada. 13 Leidse Kruisstraat. A wide variety of Spanish food.

De Groene Lanteerne (The Green Lantern). 43 Haarlemmerstraat; 241952. Three floors high, this is the narrowest restaurant in all Holland. Crowded with bric-a-brac and atmosphere.

t'Heertje. 16 Herenstraat; 251827. Authentic Dutch dishes and ambiance. Closed Wed.

Heineken's Hoek. 13 Kleine Gartmanplantsoen; 230700. Good for basic, moderately-priced lunches.

Iboya. 29 Korte Leidsedwarsstraat. Offers live entertainment as you dine.

Istanbul. 770 Keizerstraat. Fine introduction to good Turkish cooking.

Kopenhagen. 84 Rokin; 249376. For Danish snacks and meals.

La Marina. 5 Klove Niersburgwal; 222040. Spanish cuisine with a Mediterranean touch.

Mirafiori. 2 Hobbemastraat; 723013. Serving simple, but well-prepared Italian pastas and the like.

Mouwes Strictly. 73 Utrechtsestraat; 235053. Excellent for kosher sandwiches and delicatessen foods. Closed Sat.

De Oesterbar. 10 Leidseplein; 232988. A must for fish-fiends. Wide range of seafood as well as prices.

De Orient. 21 van Baerlestraat; 734958. Worth trying for something different Oriental-style.

Die Port van Cleve. 178–180 N.Z. Voorburgwal; 244860. Fine Dutch herring dishes.

Restaurant Speciaal. 89 Leliestraat; 249706. Oriental restaurant serving excellent *Rijstafel.*

Roses Cantina. 38 Reguliersdwarsstraat; 259797. Lively Mexican restaurant.

Sam Sebo. 27 P.C. Hoofstraat; 249706. Thoroughly recommended for its authentic Oriental *Rijstafel.* Closed Sun.

Sluizer. 45 Utrechtsestraat; 263557. Fish specialties. Popular.

Toga. 128 Weteringschans, for excellent Japanese *sukiyaki* and *tempura* menus.

Inexpensive

Bredero Pannekoekenhuisje. 244 O.Z. Voorburgwal; 229461. Pancakes of all sorts. Closed Tues.

Floreat. 502 Overtoom; 189129. Wide variety of attractive vegetarian dishes.

Golden Temple. 126 Utrecherstr; 268560. Macrobiotic food served with honey muffins.

HaringhandelVisser. Muntplein Haringkar. Typical Dutch herring delights served from characteristic herring cart. Closed Sun. and Mon.

t'Haringhuis. 18 Oude Doelenstraat; 221284. Another herring cart. Closed Sun. and Mon.

Leto. 114 Haarlemmerstraat. Budget food in a lively setting where the waiters create a floorshow of sorts.

Bars

Bols Taverne. 106 Rozengracht. For Bols and many other characteristic Dutch drinks; interesting.

Cafe Americain. 97 Leidsekade. Popular meeting place in the Hotel Americain.

Cafe Gollem. 4 Raamsteeg. The perfect place for beer lovers; has over 80 different beers.

't Lootsje. 103 Rozengracht. Open by appointment only, 10–2, Mon.–Fri., 10–12 Sat. Well worth making the effort to see this place, a delightful mid-17th-century house, to sample Bols.

Wijnand Fockink. 31 Pijlsteeg. Just east of the Dam at right angles to Warmoesstraat, you'll find this narrow alley. Turn in under the doorway with the naked Bacchus and the date 1679 on it, and you'll discover a pint-sized bar with a drinks list that staggers the imagination. Ask for a *half-en-halfje* (don't inquire too closely as to the contents). When it comes in its cone-shaped glass, don't pick it up but bend down and sip it, at least for the first time around—traditionalists are very firm on this point!

Brown Cafes

Among the best of these colorful Amsterdam institutions are:

Cafe Nol. 109 Westerstraat.

Dokterje. 4 Rozenboomsteeg.

De Egelantier. 72 Egelantiersgracht.

De Pilsener Club. 4 Begijnensteeg.

 NIGHTLIFE. The nightclubs of Amsterdam have now become much more daring than those in Paris and more notorious than those in Hamburg. Some say they are more exciting in every sense of the word than in any other city. To the tourist they present a strange anomaly, because while on the one hand the Dutch have always been noted for a strict morality verging on puritanism, they are also stern upholders of absolute freedom. The wide wave of sex freedom has certainly engulfed Amsterdam, where its effects are seen not only in the most bawdy nightclubs presenting every type of live show, but also in a rash of porno shops.

Amsterdam's red light district remains one of its chief sexy attractions with scantily-clad girls displaying their charms in bright windows by day and night under the unobtrusive eye of the police. This scene attracts the curious onlooker as well as the participant.

Although the police vice squad tries to stop the most daring of the nightlife attractions, they close their eyes to most of them: indeed, the fact that the most bizarre of them change their location every week or so (from bar to bar, or from houseboat to houseboat) makes police vigilance largely impossible.

For obvious reasons, most of the way-out places do not advertise their location, and sources of information are the usual world-wide ones: hotel porter, taxi driver, head barman or waiter, who will certainly require a tip of, say Fl. 5. But beware—you may find yourself in a "live" show that just might shock you beyond your wildest expectations! Amsterdam also has a number of regular gay meeting places, many of them in and near the Kerkstraat, in which the hetero-sexual has been increasingly accepted during recent years. In Holland, homosex-uality is anything but frowned on.

Although at night private rooms become public bars and some discos (such as *Atalaya,* 7 Gartmanplantsoen, *Juliana's,* 3 Breitnerstraat and *Toy-Toy* in Prinsengracht) offer more than they appear to, Amsterdam's real nightlife is concentrated in two areas: the Leidseplein and Rembrandtsplein which have a chain of dinner-cum-dancing-cum-floorshow joints. The big clubs advertise themselves well, but the best fun is obtained at the intimate bars and cabarets.

All the nightclubs and bars within the three areas mentioned above can be regarded as safe for the tourist in a physical sense, though some may make heavy demands on your purse. The same goes for places recommended by your hotel porter. Wandering off on your own down side streets and back alleys is another matter, and one should be wary about touring the more insalubrious areas at night, especially those where the drug scene is active. This applies particularly to the area around the Central Station.

The regular nightclubs listed below are generally acceptable to all but the primmest of maiden aunts (although some go in for fairly spectacular strip-tease), and are as daring as the average person would want. Most are open from about 10 P.M. to 2 A.M. or even 4 A.M. and serve drinks which are not usually excessive in price. You may find, however, that one of them might have moved or changed its name, so check your choice with your hotel porter or even with the VVV. The list below is in alphabetical order, and not necessarily in order of merit or price.

Bamboo Bar, 64 Lange Leidsedwarsstraat. Informal, inexpensive, relaxing and international. Has the longest bar in Amsterdam.

Blue Note, Leidseplein. One of the best and most respectable, even though occasionally daring. Many specialty acts, sometimes a topless girls' band, and discreet lady friends available. Open until 4 A.M.

Carrousel, 20 Thorbeckeplein. Informal, attended by the top people. Waiters are prone to jokes, while there are unannounced turns as well as a regular floorshow. Take your own instrument along if you have it, for you will be welcomed as a player.

King's Club, Korte Leidsedwarsstraat. Intimate, plush disco; not really a club.

Louis Seize, 88 Reguliersdwarsstraat. Strip shows, international variety cabaret and dancing.

De Amstel Taverne, Halvemaansteeg, close to Rembrandtsplein, a lively, pleasant gay bar with music.

AMSTERDAM AS AN
EXCURSION CENTER

Holland in a Nutshell

There are few parts of the Netherlands that offer the variety of landscape and human activity that is characteristic of the region north and south of Amsterdam. Within the span of a single day you can roll the centuries back from Dudok's modern City Hall at Hilversum to a 13th-century castle at Muiden, from the cosmopolitan glamor of Zandvoort's North Sea beach to the dreamy lassitude of Hoorn on the IJsselmeer. You can feast the eye with field after field of flowers, soothe the spirit with solitary walks through the west coast dunes, pursue the ghost of Frans Hals through the streets of Haarlem, and marvel at the wonder of a dike that stretches across open water for 32 km. (20 miles).

31

Though you would miss much of interest if you left Holland after visiting no more than this corner of the country, there is no other district that so well merits four or five days of your time. For this is the Netherlands in a nutshell, the Holland of storybook villages, peaceful fishing ports, green meadows, tiled rooftops. The flat horizon broken by windmills and distant spires, the scudding clouds chasing their reflection along the motionless surface of a canal, the fresh scrubbed farmhouses, all serve as reminders of the eternal struggle between land and sea, between man and nature.

There are so many impressions, in fact, and so much to see that you must beware of rushing. The four excursions described in the chapter are ambitious in terms of places to visit and things to do. However, most hotels and restaurants are invariably cheaper as you radiate out from Amsterdam, which means that your budget will prove more flexible.

In the province of Noord (North) Holland are Amsterdam and the principal places we are about to visit, while the bulbfields lie in the province of Zuid (South) Holland as well. With the latter, described in later chapters, its economic and political influence has been so great through the centuries that its name has become synonymous for the nation as a whole. The country's official name, of course, is *Nederland* or the Netherlands, just as the language spoken by its citizens is officially called Nederlands. However, the name Holland has come to be accepted in general use, even as the word Dutch is accepted much more universally than it was some years ago. Admittedly, however, there is apt to be some confusion because the two Provinces known as North Holland and South Holland are not geographically in the north and south of the country respectively. Yet, somehow or other, it all works itself out once you get into it.

The province of Noord Holland that we plan to explore extends from the vast dike that encloses the IJsselmeer all the way south to a line that runs very roughly from the North Sea resort of Zandvoort east to Hilversum and then back up to the IJsselmeer again, thus encircling Amsterdam, the principal city and the capital of the country. For the sake of convenience, the island of Texel has been added to the northern limit of this territory and so have the bulbfields to the south, in the companion province of Zuid Holland.

Centuries ago there was no break between this peninsula and the mass of Friesland province on the far side of the IJsselmeer, which was then, as now, a lake. The city of Hoorn, for example, was once the capital of West Friesland though only 40 km. (25 miles) separate it from Amsterdam today. Little by little, however, the sea opened larger and larger breaches in the dunes that once continued north as far as the coast of Denmark. Erosion being a progressive process, the destruction of land proceeded at an even faster pace until West Friesland lay separated from the rest of Friesland by a water gap that was 16 km. (10 miles) wide at its narrowest. Had human ingenuity been unable to arrest this trend, the map of Noord Holland would look quite different today.

With modern skills and technology, however, the sea has been driven back. The first step was the completion of an enclosing dike in 1932 that turned the Zuiderzee into a lake, which has been rechristened the IJsselmeer. With the sea held at bay to the northwest, work has progressed on empoldering—diking off and pumping dry—the pear-shaped body of fresh water that was left to the south and east. The Noordoostpolder was completed in 1942 and is fully settled. The Oostelijk Flevoland Polder came dry in the spring of 1957 and is already under cultivation. The Zuidelijk (Southern) Flevoland Polder was pumped dry by 1968 and is also already cultivated. A start has been made on the Markerwaard Polder which is turning the present harbors of Volendam, Marken, Edam and Hoorn into small lakes and completely changing their economy.

Just as nature doomed these former Zuiderzee seaports by silting up the IJsselmeer, man is now completing the process by pumping out the water. Without an understanding of the ecological transformation that is at work, the rise and decline of the cities in this region would seem arbitrary and irrational. Place these historical and natural forces in perspective, however, and a drama unfolds that is unique in Europe.

Exploring the Amsterdam Region

As already noted, distances in this part of the Netherlands are relatively so small that the region can be explored almost at will. For the sake of convenience, however, it is useful to divide our sightseeing into four itineraries, each roughly equivalent to what can be seen in a day, departing from and returning to Amsterdam. It might be helpful first to read the earlier section outlining a four-day itinerary around the IJsselmeer.

The first takes us north up the east side of North Holland along the edge of the IJsselmeer to Volendam, Marken, Edam, Hoorn, Enkhuizen, Medemblik, and on as far as the enclosing dike. The second also runs north, but up the west or ocean coast through Zaandam and Alkmaar to Den Helder and the island of Texel. The third changes direction and heads south to Aalsmeer, then west to the bulbfields, and finally back via Haarlem. The fourth turns east towards Muiden, Naarden, Hilversum, Breukelen, and the Loosdrecht Lakes (dipping here briefly into the province of Utrecht). Readers who plan to drive around the IJsselmeer can include the first and fourth itineraries as part of that trip.

1—AMSTERDAM NORTH TO VOLENDAM, HOORN, AND THE ENCLOSING DIKE

Formerly the first stage of our 216-km. (134-mile) trip was by water, taking the ferry from Amsterdam across the IJ River to the main highway leading north. Today, however, we may drive over the Schellingwoude Bridge that spans the river to the northeast or use the underwater tunnel.

Broek in Waterland is a scant 11 km. (7 miles) up the road. It seems more like a child's playground than a serious-minded community, perhaps because everything seems to be on a miniature scale. Still, it's one of the many towns where so-called Edam cheeses are produced, and if you are passing through in the summertime, you can watch them being made in the farmhouse of Jakob Wiedermeier & Son, just opposite the 15th-century church.

Hardly is the salty odor of curing cheeses out of the air than the towers of Monnikendam's Grote Kerk (Great Church) and Speeltoren signal our next stop. If it's a few minutes before the hour, hasten to the latter, which is the tower of the 18th-century town hall. Instead of bells, a carillon chimes while knights perform a solemn march. Unless they're stuck again. Take another moment to stroll down an avenue of dainty gabled houses to the harbor, and then, on your way back, note the finely detailed 17th-century Waag or Weigh House which is now a restaurant, offering smoked eels as a specialty.

Returning to the main highway long enough to cross an inlet of the IJsselmeer, we turn right at the first opportunity and ride along the top of the sea dike into Volendam, the hub of tourism in this much-frequented region. A Roman Catholic village in contrast to the Protestant fishermen on the island of Marken to the south, Volendam makes a business out of wearing traditional costumes and encouraging tourists to take pictures. Assuming that other tourists don't block your view, you can stare to your heart's content without hurting anyone's feelings, a situation that is quite different in other parts of the Netherlands.

The men sport baggy black pantaloons that are fastened with silver guilders instead of buttons. Over these are worn red-and-white-striped jackets and a cap. The women, in turn, have the appearance of birds in flight, thanks to the pointed wings on their white lace bonnets. It is rumored that some of these caps are now made of drip-dry, no-iron nylon, but no one will admit such sacrilege, yet. Be on the lookout for the *zevenkleurige rok* or seven-colored skirt, which, however ungentlemanly the advice, is better viewed from behind than in front. On Sundays a different costume is worn that is more elaborate than the workaday variety.

Connected to the mainland by a three-kilometer-long (two miles) causeway is Marken, another fishing village given a new outlook on life by the encroaching dikes that have now absorbed the island into the Markerwaard Polder. The open water, however, has been turned into a lake which will continue to attract visitors. The contrast between Volendam and Marken is greater than the distance separating them would seem to make possible. Despite the comment of one expert that "the baggy knee breeches of the Markenaars give them the look of boatmen from Greece," the effect is more Oriental than Mediterranean. The women's flowered chintzes, inspired by the East Indies, are one reason for the impression. The children, dressed alike in skirts up to the age of six, are another puzzle, and you find yourself unconsciously trying to separate brothers from sisters by some other means. The answer—boys have blue skirts.

Besides costumes, one of the chief attractions here are the houses that line Marken's narrow streets. Seafaring traditions have obviously influenced their construction, with the result that the interiors are as compact and tidy as the cabin of a ship. This nautical overtone has been muted, however, by the porcelain, clocks, glassware, hangings, and other furnishings that have been passed down from generation to generation.

Similarly, look inside the church, where model ships in full sail hang from the ceiling. Remember that Marken, a strict Reformed community, observes the Sabbath to the letter.

Instead of getting to Marken along the causeway, you might like to leave your car at Volendam and take a motorlaunch. The trip along the waterfront, lined with old Dutch houses and shops, takes about 25 minutes one way.

Back at Volendam, we continue north 5 km. (3 miles) more along the top of the sea dike to Edam, a picturesque and tranquil little town with a population of 22,000. The center is crossed by canals that have drawbridges and are lined with old houses that boast lovely façades. Edam was once an important port, but today it is best known for its cheese, which is famous all over the world for its distinctive ball-like shape and red skin. These are the characteristics of the exported variety; in Holland Edam cheese is sold with a yellow skin. It is, in fact, produced in a number of provinces. First stop, perhaps, in Edam should be the fascinating Captain's House on the Dam just opposite the

Town Hall. Paintings that hang on the walls of its front room will introduce you to some of the town's more remarkable citizens. Most imposing is the lifesize, full-length portrait of Trijntje Kester who was nearly 4 meters (13 feet) tall at the age of seventeen. Pieter Dirksz is equally arresting, thanks to a forked red beard so long that he had to fold it over his arm. Although this tonsorial triumph was possibly a handicap under some circumstances, it didn't prevent his election as mayor.

As you clamber up and down the narrow stairs, peer into the bunk-like beds built into the walls, and stand on the "bridge" with its view of the rooms below, the custodian will show you one after another item of daily usage back in the 18th century. When you are beginning to wonder how eccentric even a sea captain could be, you will be shown a cellar that literally floats, independently of the house itself.

The 18th-century Town Hall that faces this remarkable building has a green and gold council chamber that ranks it among the most beautiful of all Holland's civic rooms.

The original Grote Kerk, or Great Church, dating from the 15th century, was almost completely destroyed by fire and had to be rebuilt in 1602. It has a stately charm and some unusually fine stained-glass windows, and has now been fully restored and reopened to the public.

Another great attraction is the bell tower that carries a lovely carillon. This tower was once part of a Protestant church that was destroyed. The tower was left standing, but only just, for a few years ago it began to lean dangerously. The area was evacuated and the tower made safe. It still leans a bit, but not so much as its counterpart in Pisa. The carillon was cast in Mechelen in 1561, and is one of the oldest in the country.

Hoorn, Ancient Shipping Center

Leaving Edam, you rejoin the main north-south highway and speed along the 18 km. (11 miles) that separate it from Hoorn. You can also continue to follow the sea dike from Edam to Hoorn, but its twistings and turnings require three times as long to navigate, and the day is getting on.

Don't rush through Hoorn, however. It is certainly not a "dead city"—at least there's nothing ghostlike about the 26,000 people who live there today—and who can tell what its future will be when the Markerwaard Polder places it in the midst of rich farm country? Still, its development was abruptly arrested in the 17th century when England, not limited to flat-bottomed boats that could clear the sandbanks of the IJsselmeer, eclipsed Holland in the shipping trade. In a sense the city went to sleep, thus enabling the visitor to step three hundred years backwards in time to when Hoorn sent her ships around the world.

Willem Cornelis Schouten (1580–1625) was born here. In 1616 he was the first to round the southern tip of South America, which he named Cape Hoorn (later Horn) in honor of his home town. Another native, Jan Pieterszoon Coen (1587–1629) founded Batavia (now Jakarta), in Java, governed the island from 1617 to his death, and did much to establish Holland's empire in the East Indies. Later, Abel Janszoon Tasman (1603–59) circumnavigated Australia, discovered New Zealand, and gave his name to the island of Tasmania. Here, too, on October 11, 1573, the combined fleets of Hoorn, Enkhuizen, Edam, and Monnikendam defeated a Spanish force within sight of the ramparts and brought the Spanish Admiral Bossu back a prisoner.

As you enter the town and drive along the Kleine Noord, the 15th-century Noorderkerk (North Church) St. Mary's is on your left. A carved panel inside dated 1642 has a horn on each side, the one separating the words *wilt* and *'t-woort,* the other *gaat* and *'t-woort.* Since Hoorn is pronounced the same as *horen* (the verb "hear"), the inscription is a pun: "Be willing to hear the Word," and "Go hear the Word."

In a moment you enter the Rode Steen or Kaasmarkt, the chief square, with a statue of the aforementioned Coen in the middle, the 1609 Waag or Weigh House on the left. This is another of Hendrick de Keyser's buildings; today it houses a restaurant. The 1632 Westfries Museum is on the right. Its gable is decorated with the coats-of-arms of the seven cities of West Friesland whose delegates once sat here, while in its basement are Bronze Age artifacts and a collection of contemporary naive paintings by regional artists.

A lovely fireplace is to be found in the Grote Voorzaal, the hall, as well as several fine guild paintings. A collection of antiques and artifacts of great beauty are exhibited on the first floor, brought here during the 17th century by the East India Company, and there is also a portrait of Admiral de Ruyter by Bol (1667). In addition, there are weapons, armor, silver, porcelain, flags, coins, and much else associated with the history of Hoorn and its region. The whole of the second floor is dedicated to the maritime past of the town.

Turn left down the Grote Oost street, lined by houses whose façades incline perilously forward, perhaps to keep the rain off passers-by, perhaps to flatter the vanity of owners who wanted the ornate fronts to be more easily seen. At the end on the right, just before you cross the canal, are three houses with a frieze that re-creates the sea battle in which Bossu was defeated. Continue across the bridge through Kleine Oost to the East Gate, completed in 1578, the house on top dating from 1601. An inscription in Latin reads: "Neither the watchfulness of the guards, nor the arms, nor the threatening walls, nor the thunder of the hoarse cannon will avail anything, if thou, God, wilt not rule and shelter this town."

Retrace your steps down the Kleine Oost, cross the bridge again, and this time turn left along Slapershaven. Directly ahead is another bridge and, beyond, a house with an unusual façade and 1624 over the door. Next door is the meeting place of the West India Company in 1784.

Recross the bridge, turn left, and follow Oude Doelenkade around the curve of the inner harbor, and you'll see the remarkable tower of the Hoofdtoren, part of the harbor defences of the town and dating from 1532. The belfry on top was added 119 years later. During the 17th century it housed the offices of a company that financed whaling expeditions to the Arctic, a theme commemorated in a carved oak chimney-piece that is now in the Westfries Museum.

Returning to the central square, we head down Nieuwstraat a short block to Kerkplein. On the left at No. 39 is the Sint Jansgasthuis or St. John's Hospital, a beautiful early Renaissance building with the date 1563, which housed the ill and infirm for more than three hundred years. At the next left-hand corner of Nieuwstraat and Nieuwsteeg is the Town Hall with not one but two stepped gables. A Hieronymite convent was established here in 1385, traces of which can be identified in the present 1613 structure. The magnificent Council Room inside is enlivened with a painting representing the naval victory over Bossu.

From here we turn half-left down Gouw, then left again on Ge-dempte Turfhaven (Filled-in Peat-harbor), until we see a block away on the right, the entrance to Sint Pietershof with the date 1691. Go inside for an impression of one of the most charming of Holland's many almshouses or old people's homes. A convent antedating 1461 once stood here, then an old men's home. In 1639 it was united with an old women's home, and is still in use.

A craft market is held in Hoorn every Wednesday during the summer months. Here the visitor can watch the local craftsmen at work. Stalls are arranged around the market place and there is ample space to see the blacksmith, glassblower, glass painter, lacemaker, basket-weaver, brass worker, sculptor and many others demonstrating their traditional skills.

Enkhuizen and the Zuiderzee Museum

Another 19 km. (12 miles) bring us to a second IJsselmeer port that has declined from roughly 30,000 souls in the 17th century to about 13,000 today. Enkhuizen's herring fleet once numbered 400 vessels, setting sail not far from the massive double tower called the Drommedaris or Dromedar (1540) whose carillon ranks next to that of Edam. Of interest are the 1688 Town Hall, with a museum on the second floor, and the Stedelijk Waagmuseum, built in 1559, situated at the Kaasmarkt (cheese market). It is the old Weigh House in which cheese and butter auctions took place. Today it is a small municipal museum. We then continue to the waterside and the Zuiderzeemuseum (Binnenmuseum), appropriately lodged in the Peperhuis, a former warehouse of the East India Company. Here have been gathered together exhibits that explain much about the fishing, furniture, costumes, architecture, and topography of the entire region that today bears the name of the IJsselmeer. When you have admired the heavy timbers and solid workmanship of the three-centuries-old building, when you've studied the sample rooms with their authentically dressed dummies, when you've marveled over the manner of men who used cannon-size shotguns to decimate a flight of geese, step out the back door and examine the boats and yachts of all periods that are tied up at the pier to illustrate the history of shipbuilding. A large covered hall of ships is continuously being added to with new finds, proving that for centuries, even from Roman times, the IJsselmeer has been the graveyard of ships of all sizes and types. Holland's great problem now is to find space in which to display what are undoubtedly remarkable historical and archeological discoveries. The Wapenmuseum, or Museum of Weapons, has been established in the old prison, which has a picturesque façade dating from 1612.

The newest, and perhaps greatest, touristic achievement in Enkhuizen is the open-air Zuiderzeemuseum. Original buildings, farmhouses, shops, public offices and even a church have been collected from villages and towns around the old Zuiderzee and reerected along the cobbled streets of this museum, which was only opened in 1983 by the Queen. You reach the Zuiderzeemuseum by boat.

On the west edge of town the main road leads left. We keep straight ahead, however, following the signs for Bovenkarspel and Grootebroek. At Hoogkarspel we turn right and follow the country roads north for a total of 21 km. (13 miles) to Medemblik, the third and smallest of our dreaming IJsselmeer cities. We now pass the restored Radboud Castle, which was built in the 8th century by the Frisian King Radboud. In 1288 Count Floris V fortified the castle to keep his recently-conquered Frisian subjects from rebelling. Only part of the building was destroyed in the 17th and 18th centuries. The castle houses a small collection of coins and antiques.

We now continue to 25 Westerhaven. From the outside, this appears to be just another fine home, but inside there is a winter stable with animal pens, haystack, and all. In summer, following the old West Frisian custom, the cattle live in the fields (sometimes wearing canvas "coats" if the weather is chilly). The house, owned by the Schouten brothers, is used for displaying antiques. Visitors are welcome.

In other respects, Medemblik falls short of Hoorn and Enkhuizen. As you leave town by the Medemblikkerweg leading northwest to the main highway, keep your eye cocked for the Lely pumping station on the right at some distance from the road. We are now entering the Wieringermeer Polder, completed in 1930, and it was one of the two stations used to pump the water out. It has the unbelievable capacity of 1,500,000 litres (330,000 gallons) per *minute,* yet when you consider that much of the 20,235 hectares (50,000 acres) reclaimed here are 6 meters (18 feet) below sea level, the need for such a vast potential becomes evident.

Three towns were built in the midst of this pentagon-shaped polder: Slootdorp, Middenmeer, and Wieringerwerf. The highway leads us past the last of these, about 6 km. (4 miles) west of the point where the Germans breached the dike on April 17, 1945, only 18 days before the Nazi surrender. The land, of course, was completely flooded, but the polder was pumped dry as soon as the dike had been repaired, and, thanks to the fact that the IJsselmeer is today nearly 100% fresh, crops were growing again in the fields by the following spring.

Twenty-three kilometers (14 miles) after leaving Medemblik we pass a second pumping station at the northern end of Wieringermeer Polder and cross a corner of the former island of Wieringen to the town of Den Oever, the beginning of the Afsluitdijk or enclosing dike.

The late author Karel Capek made such projects seem elementary. "You take a bit of sea," he wrote, "fence it and pump it out, and at the bottom is left a deposit to which a very respectable slice of Europe, by means of its rivers, supplies its best swampy soil, and the sea finest sand; the Dutchman drains it, and sows grass there, the cows feed on it, the Dutchman milks them, and thus makes cheese, which at Gouda or Alkmaar is sold to England . . . "

It is the enclosing dike that makes this all so simple. Although many men dreamed of running a barrier from Noord Holland to Friesland and reclaiming the IJsselmeer, Dr. Lely was the first to conceive a practical plan, back in 1891. Persuading the government to appropriate the funds required an additional 25 years. Actual work commenced in 1923. The dike you see today is 29 km. (18 miles) long, 92 meters (300 feet) wide, and 6 meters (21 feet) above mean water level. Its top carries a surfaced motor road plus a path for bicycles and another for pedestrians. Sheep are grazed on the grass strips in between.

Slightly more than halfway across, a monument raises its tower above the point at which the dike was closed on May 28, 1932. From its top you can survey the entire project from shore to shore on a fine day, and, if the daring of the scheme has caught your imagination, buy an illustrated booklet describing this and a number of other reclamation plans. Then, turning back after a pause at the café in the base of the monument, we start the 89-km. (55-mile) run back to Amsterdam.

But the Dutch have found more than romance and history in their old IJsselmeer. Apart from the large areas of new land being reclaimed from that historic basin of water, they are now using it for hydraulic studies as well. On the eastern side, near Emmen, the Delft Hydraulics Laboratory has established a large open-air and covered experimental station in which extensive model studies are carried out not only for current and planned Dutch projects but also for hydraulic works intended for countries all over the world.

II—AMSTERDAM NORTHWEST TO ZAANDAM, ALKMAAR, AND TEXEL

This excursion is shorter than the first—183 km. (114 miles)—and takes us up the west coast of Noord Holland to Den Helder, terminus for the boats to Texel (which there won't be time to visit in a single day), then back down through the center of the province to Amsterdam. We are completely away from the IJsselmeer with its memories of days of glory.

We leave Amsterdam by the road that leads to Zaanstad, via the Coentunnel underneath the Noordzee Kanaal or North Sea Canal, another of the mighty engineering works of the Dutch. You'll recall that originally Amsterdam's ships reached the open sea by sailing east to the IJsselmeer and then north. The silting of the IJsselmeer during the 18th century, however, threatened Amsterdam (where during the Golden Age more than 3,000 ships could be counted alongside the busy quays) with extinction unless some new outlet were discovered that could accommodate vessels of deep draft. The North Sea Canal was the solution.

Extending for 24 km. (15 miles) through dunes whose average height is 10 meters (33 feet) above sea level, it reaches the ocean at the fishing village of IJmuiden after passing through a set of locks so vast that the *QE 2* could pass through with 45 meters (150 feet) to spare at each end. The canal itself was opened in 1876 after 11 years of labor; the present system of locks was completed in 1930 and can cope with a difference in water level of 4 meters (13 feet), although the average is normally about half that. So much salt water is admitted every time the locks are used that the entire IJsselmeer could be contaminated if there were not another set of locks at the Amsterdam end to keep the waterway isolated. The entrance was recently enlarged to accommodate tankers.

For many years the canal had the effect of cutting Noord Holland in half and leaving road traffic dependent on ferries. In 1957, however, a vehicular tunnel was completed in Velsen, while more recently the Coentunnel and the IJ tunnel were finished, giving Amsterdam better connections with northern parts.

The Zaan area, which we enter after crossing the canal, was Holland's great windmill area centuries ago, and although hundreds have been torn down, having been replaced by modern pump engines, you will still see a few scattered here and there. Even more important, if you play golf, is the fact that the district gave birth to the game of *kolf,* the lineal ancestor of today's pastime. There is little resemblance to today's game; then only one club was used which looked like a rather unfortunate combination of hockey stick and polo mallet. The ball, a clumsy leather affair, was half again bigger than a cricket ball or soft ball. You can see some of these primitive implements, by the way, at Den Haag Golf and Country Club.

During the 17th century Holland was renowned as the leading ship-building nation of the world, with Zaandam as its center. One of the many people who came here to study Dutch progress in ship-building, mathematics and physics at first hand was Peter the Great, the enlightened young Czar of All the Russias. Arriving "incognito" in Zaandam in 1697, he worked in the shipyards as Peter Michailov, but local curiosity forced him to take refuge in Amsterdam after one week. Czar Nicholas II (1868–1918) arranged to have the small wooden house his ancestor had inhabited during his short stay in Zaandam turned into a museum, now called Het Czaar-Peterhuisje, and in 1911 he presented the town with a statue of Czar Peter, which now adorns the marketplace.

A few kilometers up the road we come to Koog aan de Zaan, notable chiefly for the old (1751) Het Pink windmill, which has been converted into a museum specializing in the history and construction of mills. At Zaandijk, a village just east of the highway, is an antiquities museum, housed in the 18th-century home of a wealthy merchant. Its rooms are furnished in the typical old *Zaanse* style and represent the life, culture and industry of the district in former times. Even more interesting is the Zaanse Schans plan which is an old windmill village. Strolling round the green Zaan houses and the windmills you'll find yourself back in the 17th century. An old mustard mill, called De Huisman, was built in 1786 as a snuff mill and is still used today to grind the "genuine Zaan Mustard". De Zoeker is the last working oil mill in the country. It shows how vegetable oil is pressed out of oil-seeds or oil nuts.

This Zaan area, however, has not escaped the Dutch industrial revolution. Side by side with the old buildings still redolent of clever craftsmanship there are now busy factories turning out a host of different products. Yet every effort is being made to retain some of the old-time glamor of the area.

We continue up the main road beyond Wormerveer to Krommenie, a hamlet where everything seems to be on a miniature scale. Gables, pilasters, façades, cornucopias, and sculptured panels abound in this arcadia of two-roomed cottages. Particularly interesting are the houses at 74 Noorder Hoofdstraat and at 65 and 115 Zuider Hoofdstraat.

If it's spring, take the Alkmaar highway and stop at Limmen, a center of the tulip, narcissus, and hyacinth industry, where there is a unique outdoor "tulip museum" in which practically all the original varieties of this wonderful flower are still preserved—and grown. If not, turn north at Uitgeest and follow the country road to Akersloot, the oldest village in this part of the Netherlands according to records that date back to 777. Even more impressive, however, is the Alkmaarder Lake on which it lies, a yachting center crowded with graceful craft. Beyond Akersloot the road follows the west side of a canal all the way into Alkmaar.

Alkmaar and its Cheese Market

Though Alkmaar is famous today for the Friday-morning cheese market (end of April to end of September), it is worth visiting in its own right, too. Its origins go back to the 12th century, but its proudest day was in 1573 when Don Frederico of Toledo, son of the dreaded Duke of Alva, was forced to abandon his siege of the town. This was the first important victory over the Spanish, the first indication that the Dutch could hope to succeed in throwing off the foreign yoke.

The late 15th-century St. Laurenskerk (St. Lawrence's Church) has one of the finest antique organs in the Netherlands, not to mention the tomb of Count Floris V, who overcame the fierce Frisians and built the castle we saw yesterday at Medemblik. The Town Hall, a beautiful Gothic building from 1520, contains a fine collection of porcelain. The Stedelijk Museum is in a historic building, Nieuwe Doelen, built in the early 16th century and housing a collection of old toys, maps and pictures of Alkmaar's past. But the glory of Alkmaar is the Waaggebouw or Weigh House. As you stand below its ornate step gables, your eye is drawn upward by a labyrinth of receding planes that culminate in the weathervane. If the hour is about to strike, pause for a moment to enjoy the chimes and watch the moving figures. Then climb the tower for a view of the town that takes you back three hundred years and more.

If it's a Friday morning, it won't be easy to tear yourself from the spectacle taking place at your feet. The cheeses arrive at the market by barge (the factory may be as little as one kilometer away), and are unloaded by means of a juggling act that would do credit to any circus as the round balls, weighing 2–6.5 kg. (4–14 lb.), are pitched from the barge to barrows that look vaguely like stretchers. At this point the porters or carriers take over. Together they form an ancient guild with the exclusive privilege of handling the cheeses. A "father" directs the activities of the 28 porters and various older workers who assist them. The porters, in turn, are divided into four groups or *veems*. Each group consists of three pairs of carriers and a silver-badged headman who is responsible for seeing that his men are spotless, punctual, and well disciplined, and that the group's scales are correct.

The actual selling of the cheeses takes place in a ring and is consummated by a handclasp that is as binding on both parties as a signed contract. The porters wait until a barrow is piled high with cannonball-sized cheeses. They then attach a leather shoulder sling to the barrow's handles and jog off with a distinctive bobbing gait calculated not to spill the load. At the weighroom the barrow is set on the group's own scales. The total is noted on a blackboard, and then the barrow is carried off to the new owner of the cheeses or, more likely, his barge.

All morning long the twelve pairs of porters jog their way through the crowds of tourists to the Waggebouw, or Weigh House, and back, gradually building up their tally for the day. The color group with the highest total is made chief guild group until the following week. When the market is over, the porters retire to their own quarters to drink beer specially brewed for the occasion, using centuries-old pewter mugs that have been handed down from father to son. Over the fireplace hangs a "shame board" with the names of the men who were late reporting to work or who cursed while on duty. The Waggebouw was once a Chapel of the Holy Ghost, built at the end of the 14th century, which served as a refuge for needy travelers. It was transformed into a Weigh House in 1582 after Alkmaar's weighing rights were restored.

During the Kaasmarkt, the 35-bell carillon bursts into life with a medley of popular and classical tunes that cascade down the belfry in a golden shower. As a glorious finale, the noon hour is announced, and at every stroke of the bell, a trumpeter blows his horn, doors open, and horsemen burst out of the clock tower, lances held high.

For 300 years cheese has been sold in this fashion at Alkmaar. If today the market is perpetuated for the benefit of tourists (more efficient ways of handling cheese have been developed over the centuries), it is done with a zest that betrays the townspeople's own delight in recalling bygone days when there was time for pageantry.

Leaving Alkmaar we turn half-left off the main highway to the pleasant village of Bergen, which lies on the edge of the sea dunes and beside a forest. For the last hundred years or so, various schools of Dutch artists have settled here where life is pleasant and cheap and the surroundings inspiring. In summer they hang their canvases under the shady trees, adjourn to a nearby café, and await the call of fame and fortune. Roughly 5 km. (3 miles) due west is Bergen-aan-Zee, a simple, family-type seaside resort similar to Egmond-aan-Zee and Castricum-aan-Zee, which lie farther down the coast to the south.

We follow a local road north, however, towards Schoorl, skirting the edge of the widest and most densely wooded dunes in the Netherlands. We pass through sleepy villages—Bregtdorp, Katrijp, Hargen, Camperduin—that curve gently westward until suddenly we are face to face with the North Sea. Ahead of us stretches a 5-km. (3-mile) gap in the dunes that has been heavily reinforced with piles, breakwaters, and dikes with the collective name of Hondsbosse Zeewering. The road runs alongside the fortifications to Petten, which has been twice submerged by the sea.

The coastal road ducks back behind a new range of dunes for another 10 km. (6 miles) to the dreamy seaside resort of Callantsoog. From there it's a straight run into Den Helder at the northernmost tip of Noord Holland.

Den Helder and Texel Island

Bordered by the rolling North Sea on three sides, set among extensive bulb fields that bloom during April and May, and secure behind heavy dikes, Den Helder is full of surprises. At the end of the 18th century it was a forgotten fishing village visited by seagulls. Then, in January 1794, the Dutch fleet got itself frozen into the ice between Den Helder and Texel Island opposite. A detachment of French cavalry took advantage of this predicament by riding out on the ice and capturing the fleet, one of the few instances in naval warfare when horsemen have been decisive. Five years later the Duke of York landed here with a force of 13,000 Russian and 10,000 English troops, who were subsequently defeated near Bergen by French and Dutch forces based on Alkmaar. In 1811, Napoleon ordered the town fortified.

Today Den Helder is the chief Dutch naval base and training center, recruiting many men and women from the sturdy citizens of the city itself. The Royal Naval College, the Admiralty Palace, an interesting Maritime Museum, the state shipyards, and usually a contingent of vessels can be seen. Naval uniforms seem to predominate, and even the local young ladies seem to have adopted the rolling gait of the sailor. Standing on the quay you can recall that glorious day in 1673 when a

Dutch fleet under the command of admirals Tromp and De Ruyter defeated a combined English and French fleet almost within sight of this coast.

Texel, the largest—21 km. (13 miles) long, 10 (6) wide—and most southerly of the five Wadden Islands, is a scant 3 km. (2 miles) from Den Helder. A good ferry service carrying passengers and cars makes the 15-minute run to the port of 't Horntje. You might prefer to leave your car in the free parking area in front of the ferry terminal in Den Helder and take the passenger ferry which can save a long wait in the high season. On the other side there are frequent buses from the 't Horntje terminal to different parts of the island. This is also a more economical way to see the island. Less than 11,000 people live in the seven villages scattered about its surface, although during the year it has millions and millions of visitors. For Texel is a bird paradise, a breeding ground (May and June) discovered by the birds themselves and now protected by the island authorities. Its wide dunes, extensive moors, shallow lakes, and wooded clumps form ideal seasonal homes for mating, breeding, and training the young as part of that great miracle of nature known as migration. In the spring the visitors arrive by the million. Almost every known variety of duck and geese, belligerent ruffs and peaceful reeves, avocets and plovers, wagtails and warblers, stately spoonbills and dignified herons, kestrels and bitterns, gotwits and martens—these are just a few of the regulars who turn this island into a bird-lover's treasure-house. The guides who conduct the human visitors around these sanctuaries know just how far the different bird colonies will tolerate inquisitiveness. For the special benefit of bird-lovers the Texel VVV has prepared a brochure on the bird life of the island, including a survey of the different reserves and a checklist of those which can be seen. If you decide to stay here for a few days, there are a number of smallish hotels, some of which make special arrangements for bird watchers, including excursions.

But don't expect to rush around Texel. This is an isle of peace, and the visitor in a hurry is regarded as having come to the wrong place. On Texel you are expected to move quietly, to take your time to see the special flocks of sheep grazing so placidly on its pasture, or the millions of narcissi blooming in spring, or its fishing fleet, or farmers who make their special green cheese from ewe milk.

On Texel you can ride, cycle, walk, or take a bus. The seven villages are linked by good though narrow roads, and the rolling dunes and golden beaches are unhampered by restrictions on walking or bathing or picnicking.

The whole transport system of the island covering the ferry and bus services are owned by Teso which stands for Texel's Eigen Stoomboot Onderneming, meaning Texel's Own Steamship Society. Owned by the local population, it began by opening the steamer service, and the profits from its activities mainly go towards improving the roads, educational facilities and health schemes of the island. Teso runs several modern drive-on-drive-off vessels, each carrying 70 motor vehicles and 750 passengers, giving an hourly service: although in busy periods there is a trip every half hour. Reservation of space is neither necessary nor possible. Private cars are given priority so that even in the busiest times there is usually little waiting, except at Easter and the height of the summer season. The journey is a pleasant one and makes it possible to get from Amsterdam to Texel in about two hours.

Perhaps unfortunately for the foreign tourist, the Dutch have at last "discovered" Texel and the other northern islands, for weekend campouts. Another local problem is the desire of Dutch oil companies to explore the island and its surrounding waters for oil and gas, as borings have suggested that it will be as fruitful in providing new fuel sources as some areas of the adjacent North Sea.

South to Broek op Langedijk

The quickest way back to Amsterdam from Den Helder is via the main highway Alkmaar and Zaandam, which we have been following or skirting all day. Instead, let's take an extra hour or two to explore a series of country roads and the simple farming communities.

Ten kilometers (six miles) south of Den Helder a left-hand fork leads east to Anna Paulowna, a town strung along the waters of a canal that drains a polder of the same name, honoring the Russian Grand Duchess who married Willem, Prince of Orange, later King Willem II, in 1816. A sharp turn takes us south again until we join a better road at Schagen, the scene of a weekly folklore pageant during July and August. Then southeast to Oude Niedorp and to Noordscharwoude, the beginning of a remarkable 5-km. (3-mile) community that changes its name to Zuidscharwoude and then Broek op Langedijk. On the other side of the main highway, between Bergen and Heerhugowaard, you will find one of the biggest artificial ski-slopes in Europe.

This is the country of a thousand islands, a spot unique even in the rambling waterland that is Holland. A maze of canals tied together by a web of lovely bridges greets the eye, together with Frisian gondolas gliding back and forth carrying farmers and vast loads of cabbages, potatoes, and the like. Chances are they are all bound in one direction, towards the auction hall that claims to be the world's oldest (1887), largest, and most remarkable vegetable market.

Below Broek op Langedijk we rejoin a main highway for another 5 km. (3 miles). When it forks right for Alkmaar, we turn left and follow an arrowlike country road east across the middle of the Schermer

Polder, whose midpoint is marked by the village of Stompetoren. Just before entering Schermerhorn, we climb out of this polder only to descend, just beyond, into the even older (1612) Beemster Polder, perhaps the most beautiful in all Holland. This is an orchard area whose fruit trees burst into blossom between the end of April and early May. Some of the original farmhouses still stand, bearing such dates as 1682 and 1695, and can be seen on the right-hand side of the road less than two kilometers south of Midden Beemster.

Working our way east around the right-angle corners of this grid-iron-shaped paradise, we soon enter Purmerend, which stands on high ground in the middle of the Beemster, Purmer, and Wormer polders. The church, which dates back to 1358, was largely rebuilt in 1591 and has a fine baroque organ (1742), but the major attractions are the tremendous pig, cattle, and horse market on Tuesday mornings and the historical Kaasmarkt. The cheese market is centuries old and is held at the foot of the Town Hall with its fine carillon. Every Thursday, from the second in June until the third in August, Purmerend bustles with cheese-based activities. Cheese porters, dressed usually in white with only blue or red ribbon distinguishing their guild, and sporting straw hats, show the public how they taste, weigh and buy the cheese.

From Purmerend a 16-km. (10-mile) stretch of highway leads back to Amsterdam.

III—AMSTERDAM SOUTH TO AALSMEER, THE BULBFIELDS, AND HAARLEM

This is the shortest of our excursions—112 km. (70 miles) if the bulbfields are in bloom, otherwise 77 (48)—and the most beautiful. Hardly are we out of Amsterdam on the main highway leading south to Den Haag and Rotterdam than we drop down into the Haarlemmer-meer Polder, the largest and most important in the Netherlands until the enclosing dike was completed. For centuries this lake—23 km. (14 miles) long—was a constant threat to Haarlem and even Amsterdam as well as to the ships that sailed across or fished in its waters. A gale or even a sudden change of wind was enough to pile its waves against the dikes along its sides.

As early as 1617, one of Holland's most talented engineers and windmill designers, Jan Adriaansz Leeghwater, conceived a plan for diking and draining the Haarlemmer Meer. The book in which he described his scheme for using 160 windmills went through seventeen editions, but the capital investment required was too great for those days and the success of so ambitious an undertaking was too problematic. Not until 1851 with the advent of steam powered pumps did his dream become a reality.

These thoughts fresh in our mind, we turn off the main road and follow the signs pointing to Schiphol Airport, which lies located in the northeast corner of this vast polder, a circumstance that makes it unlike any other airfield in the world. To begin with, the runways are 4 meters (13 feet) below sea level, a statement you can verify as you drive along the top of the dike that keeps the polder dry.

Schiphol is the most important commercial airport in the country and one of the busiest and best-equipped airports in Europe. At Schiphol is the national aviation museum Aviodrome, with its striking aluminum dome. It contains displays depicting man's adventures in the air since the days of the Wright brothers, and contains many early planes as well as scale models of space ships.

Past the entrance to Schiphol, however, we continue along the top of the dike another 5 km. (3 miles) or so to Aalsmeer, and on past it for another mile. Then turn left to see the Centrale Aalsmeerse Bloemenveiling, the most important flower auction hall in Europe. There are five auction rooms, two for potted plants, two for cut flowers, and one for bulb flowers. Buyers begin bidding as early as 7 A.M. and continue until everything has been sold, usually about 11 or 11:30. In a single year, as many as 95 million carnations, 15 million chrysanthemums, 750 million roses, 9 million sprays of lilac, and 14 million sweet peas pass through this building, as well as thousands of other varieties, representing sales of around 400 million guilders a year.

The great majority of these are raised in 325 hectares (800 acres) of hot-houses and 1,000 nurseries run by 3,000 growers, all within a radius of two or three kilometers of the auction rooms. They arrive by barge and are sorted out into lots. A sample is selected from each lot and held up for the assembled buyers to see. The auctioneer then sets in motion what looks like a vast clock with numbers around the rim and in the middle. The numbers in the middle correspond to the seats in which the buyers sit, each of which has an electric button. The numbers around the rim represent prices for ten bunches of flowers or plants similar to the sample being displayed. A pointer, like a huge minute-hand, begins to move, but instead of starting at low prices and working up, it begins at high prices and moves backwards. The instant it reaches a price acceptable to the most eager buyer, he presses his button, the minute-hand stops, and the number of his seat lights up on the clock face. This proceeds at the rate of roughly 600 lots per hour.

Once sold, the flowers are taken to the packing and delivery sheds. Those intended for export are skilfully wrapped in tissue and lightweight cardboard boxes, rushed to nearby Schiphol Airport, and are being admired in Stockholm, Paris, and London flowershop windows before the end of the day, all within 12 hours of the time they were cut. Those for sale in Holland are loaded in trucks and dispatched to shops all over the country.

Even in the depths of winter when the roads are slick with ice and the canals half frozen, bargefuls of huge cherry chrysanthemums, roses, carnations, and lilies appear in the Aalsmeer auction room, together with a wonderful array of cyclamens and miniature azaleas, both popular as Christmas presents.

And in September when the town goes all out for its Bloemencorso or flower festival, something over two million blossoms are used for the huge decorated floats, a sight that attracts thousands of flower fanciers to Amsterdam's Olympic stadium.

Holland's Bulbfields

Still dazzled by the sight of so many flowers in one place, we retrace our route for half a kilometer or so to the edge of the Haarlemmermeer Polder, where we plunge west across its middle on a road so straight that we are through Hoofddorp or "Head Village" before we realize it. On the far side of the polder, just as the road climbs slightly to go over the western dike, a strange building on the right attracts our eye.

This is the Cruquius Pumping Station, completed in 1849, which helped pump out the Haarlemmermeer. It was in continuous use until 1933, when it was converted into a museum (Museum de Cruquius) that well merits a stop. Besides explaining by means of working models how a polder drainage system works, it contains a relief map of the entire Netherlands which can be flooded at will and then pumped dry in a vivid demonstration of the fate that would overtake the country if all the dikes were to give way or if the polar ice caps were to melt (producing a rise in sea level calculated at 49 meters, or 160 feet!). Models of various kinds of windmills can be seen here as well as a detailed explanation of how major dikes are constructed today. Don't overlook the Cruquius pump, an engineering freak with eight beams transmitting power to as many pumps from a single cylinder with 3-meter (10-foot) stroke. This freak had a capacity of 386,400 liters (85,000 gallons) per minute and operated for 84 years, so it ill behoves us to mock its forest of levers, pipes, and gauges.

The delightful garden city of Heemstede lies on the higher ground just outside the Haarlemmermeer. If the bulb season is past, we continue west to Zandvoort. Let's assume, however, that it's April or early May and turn south for Bennebroek and the most important bulbfields.

Such great progress has been made in producing new varieties of the main bulb plants that the calendar is no longer quite the tyrant it used to be. Still, there is a general progression in this part of Holland from daffodils and narcissi from the end of March to the middle of April, early tulips and hyacinths from the second week of April to the end of the month, and late tulips immediately afterwards. An early or late spring can move these approximate dates forward or backward by as much as two weeks.

The art of bulb-growing, by the way, has been a Dutch specialty since the first tulip was brought to Holland from Turkey in 1559. In 1625 an offer of 3,000 florins for two bulbs was turned down, but the speculation in bulbs became a mania during the years 1634–1637, as irrational and popular as stock market speculation in the late 1920's, when fortunes were made—and lost—in a single day. Individual bulbs worth thousands of guilders had their pictures painted in tulip books that enjoyed a similar vogue. Only during the last 60 years has the scientific approach prevailed. Today's experts diagnose the rarest tulips illustrated in the books that have survived as suffering from viruses that caused abnormal (and beautiful) coloring or shape.

The bulbfields themselves extend from just north of Leiden to the southern limits of Haarlem, but the greatest concentration is limited to the district that begins at Sassenheim and ends between Hillegom and Bennebroek. In a neat checkerboard pattern of brilliant color the fields stretch out as far as the eye can see.

The apparent artificiality of the sharply defined rectangular fields is not a concession to taste. It is part of the businesslike efficiency of an industry that has made the bulb one of Holland's most important export commodities. It must be remembered that here the bulb, not the flower, is the most important part of the plant. When the flowers are ripe, so to speak, they are cut off, leaving only the green stalks. The children play with the discarded blooms, threading them into garlands which they sell to passing motorists or use to make floral mosaics.

Let's follow the main Hillegom-Lisse-Sassenheim road south from Heemstede. At Bennebroek, just before we enter the core of the bulb district, is Linnaeushof Garden. It comes by its name honestly, for the famous 18th-century Swedish botanist once worked on these very grounds studying and classifying the plants he found in the garden of the then lord mayor of Amsterdam. Open from April to October, this garden features bulb flowers in April and May, lilies, lilacs, roses, and the like in June and July, and begonias and dahlias in August and September. It also features the Minicorso—the world's tiniest flower parade—all through the year.

Soon we are in Hillegom where we stop briefly at Treslong, the official demonstration garden of the bulb-growers, started in 1949. As many as 70,000 bulbs of 700 varieties can be seen here, each identified by name and grower. We are now in the province of Zuid, or South, Holland. While in Hillegom visit the nurseries of M. van Waveren & Sons, founded in 1822 and the largest bulb-growers in the country. In their hothouses, where the first snow-white amaryllis and pink calla lily were grown, an endless variety of new cross-strains are being developed to grace the gardens of the future. In the warehouses you can see how some of Holland's yearly 5,000,000,000 export bulbs are packed for shipment all over the world.

Between here and Sassenheim you may notice flower mosaics on one side or the other of the main road. These are worked out, petal by petal, by the local residents in competition with each other, usually reaching their peak just before the annual Bloemencorso or flower parade. This last, starting from Sassenheim, Lisse, or Hillegom (the starting point changes yearly) on the morning of the third or fourth Saturday in April, consists of a score or more floats that pass along the main highway to Haarlem, making the return trip in the afternoon. No reservations or entry fees are required. Simply arrive in ample time and station yourself along the 10-km. (6-mile) stretch of road.

Keukenhof Gardens

Lisse, the middle of the three main bulb towns, is noted for its Keukenhof Gardens, but we keep straight ahead to Sassenheim, turning right (west) into the bulbfields at the north edge of town. At Loosterweg we head north again, following the zigs and zags of this country lane as it passes through the very heart of the fields so overburdened with color. Presently we are back at Lisse again, and follow the signs for Keukenhof.

From the end of March to the end of May the 28 hectare (70 acre) Keukenhof Gardens, founded by leading bulb-growers, are a living open-air flower exhibition that is unique in the world. As many as 10 million bulbs blossom here together, either in hothouses (where they may reach a height of nearly 1 meter, or 3 feet) or in flowerbeds along the sides of a charming lake. Holland's leading bulb-growers have joined together to make this old estate a permanent treasure house of floral beauty.

This world-famed Keukenhof celebrated its 25th birthday in 1974, and although some special events were held to honor the occasion, you can always see the lively "meisjes" (girls) who stroll around as guides and hostesses in the oldtime costume of Jacoba van Beieren, who had her hunting lodge here in the 15th century, and who was in succession Dauphiness of France, Duchess of Gloucester and Countess of Bavaria.

Spring is not the only time of the year when this man-made tide of color bursts the dikes and floods the fields around Lisse. Just as the many hues of hyacinths and tulips march across the countryside in disciplined ranks during April and May, so in July and August does the stately gladiolus welcome visitors to his domain. Then, in September, the dahlia takes over by way of emphasizing the horticultural preeminence of these sandy fields by the North Sea. A further Lisse attraction is the Huys Dever, a keep dating from 1375 and providing a setting for exhibitions and concerts.

From Keukenhof, Loosterweg III leads to North Holland and to Vogelenzang, whose name means "song of the birds". Birds there are, too, in profusion, for this is the wooded edge of the dunes that next lead us due west to the cosmopolitan seaside resort of Zandvoort. Flattened to the last brick by the Germans during the building of their World War II defensive Atlantic Wall, Zandvoort has been rebuilt just back from the water's edge.

First let's drive up the coast to the 5-km. (3-mile), closed circuit for motorcycles and cars where international races are held during June and July. If you like to burn rubber yourself, you can rent the track for an hour or two and have a go at the lap record. It also accommodates the most popular anti-skid motoring school in Europe.

The coastal road turns abruptly inland a mile or so beyond the entrance to the Zandvoort track, leading us back through dunes to Bloemendaal, or Flowerdale, whose open-air theater is used by the Old Vic company, among others, in Shakespearean programs. In addition, it offers a miniature lake, botanical gardens, and an aviary.

Along the coast, within easy reach of Lisse, are a number of excellent beach resorts, large and small. The best known are Noordwijk and Zandvoort.

Haarlem, Home of the Arts

It is a short step from this ocean of annual color to a haven of perennial color. In the heart of Haarlem we find the earliest center of Dutch art. Lying in the shadow of a nest of lovely medieval buildings in the heart of this 900-year-old city of 160,000 people is the Frans Halsmuseum housing a fine collection of masterpieces by this famous Dutch painter and other artists who worked here in the 16th and 17th centuries. The building at 62 Groot Heiligland, in which the display is housed, was originally one of 25 picturesque old almshouses dotted around the lovely Groote Kerk, or Church of St. Bavo, completed in the 16th century having been under construction for over a hundred years. Known as Ouedemannenhuis, it was built largely by the Ghent architect Lieven de Key (1560–1627) and opened as the Frans Hals-museum in 1913.

The genius of Frans Hals (c.1580–1666) has not only established itself in his peerless paintings, but has also influenced such painters as Buytewech, Terborch and Brouwer. Hals is one of the finest portrait painters that Holland has ever produced, and his corporation pieces, paintings of the guilds of Haarlem, are to be admired in the museum. The setting for these arresting paintings, some amazingly virile and some unbelievably peaceful, is in itself a gem of artistry. The museum is open in the evening from the end of March until June.

In the center of Haarlem, around the great market square, the whole story of Dutch architecture can be traced in a chain of majestic buildings ranging through the 15th, 16th, 17th, 18th, and 19th centuries. With a smile and perhaps a little bravado you can enter most of them, from the Town Hall of the 14th century, with its candle-lit and tapes-tried Council Chamber, long the home of battlers for freedom, to the Meat Market, of all places, one of Holland's greatest Renaissance buildings of the beginning of the 17th century. Externally it is unique, for nowhere in the country is there such a fine sweep of stepped gables that invite you, had you a giant's stride, to clamber up to the pinnacle that almost pierces the scudding clouds. No longer does this fanciful building serve the butcher's needs. Today, it often houses the most adventurous of modern art exhibitions.

Housed in its remarkable collection of architecture, Haarlem offers a variety of museums. In the Teyler Museum, besides a fine collection of the Hague school of painting, you can see an unexpected collection of original sketches and drawings by Michelangelo, Leonardo da Vinci, Titian, Raphael and other non-Dutch masters, against a background of fossils and other petrified remains. The Episcopal Museum in Jans-straat concentrates on medieval art, particularly Catholic ecclesiastical. The Enschede Museum on Klokhuisplein houses an unusual collection telling the story of the development of printing (note the statue of Laurens Coster in Grote Markt, to whom every Haarlemmer and almost every Dutchman attributes the invention of printing), and the van Looy house in Kleine Houtweg which is the home of modern art exhibitions side by side with Jacobus van Looy's own works.

The Church of St. Bavo is girdled with souvenir shops literally growing out of its walls and buttresses. But if you can forget these unnecessary tributes to commercialism, go inside. The interior as well as the outside of this imposing structure reveals to the trained eye the architecture of three centuries. Above all, look at the organ, one of Europe's most famous, with three keyboards, 68 registers, and 5,000 pipes. Built in 1738 by C. Mueller, it has been played on by Mozart and Händel, and many modern masters of that form of music. As an expert says: "There are few buildings in the world where a Bach prelude and fugue sound more imposing than in this grandest of all Dutch churches". To prove it, organ recitals are played all through the summer on Tuesdays and Thursdays.

Spaarndam's Statue to a Legend

A couple of kilometers or so northeast of Haarlem is a statue to a legend, a statue that proves once again the power of imaginative fiction. You may recall the young boy Pieter who appears in the pages of an American book called *Hans Brinker or the Silver Skates*. The story goes that he discovered a hole in a dike one afternoon and plugged it with his finger while waiting for help to come. All night long he stood vigil until, when help finally arrived the following morning, he was dead, having heroically saved Haarlem from destruction.

So many people have asked where Pieter lived and where he performed his brave deed that the Dutch finally felt compelled to do something about the legend. In 1950 Princess Irene, accompanied by her mother Queen Juliana, unveiled a memorial, if not to Pieter, then to the courage and devotion of Dutch youth through the centuries. The place selected was Spaarndam, a choice as logical as any and more picturesque than most. Even if no dike could be saved by so puny an instrument as a boy's finger, the memorial has been cunningly placed so that the motorist who stops to admire it can plug the flow of traffic around with 100% effectiveness. Needless to say, most Dutch people, when asked, know nothing whatever about the legend. It is one of those happy fictions that has the ring of truth.

Following the signs for Zwanenburg, we rejoin the main Haarlem-Amsterdam highway, and are back in the city of canals in 20 minutes.

IV—AMSTERDAM SOUTHEAST TO MUIDEN, NAARDEN AND HILVERSUM

The last of our four Amsterdam-based trips takes us along the southern edge of the IJsselmeer to the garden district of Gooiland, a 120-km. (75-mile) excursion that reaches into what is technically Utrecht Province long enough to see the Queen Mother's palace at Soestdijk, Queen Beatrix' palace of Drakenstein at Lage Vuursche where she lived until she moved to Den Haag after her Coronation, and the costume villages of Spakenburg and Bunschoten, and the pleasant woodland town of Baarn.

First stop is Muiden, 18 km. (11 miles) east of Amsterdam, whose castle, Muiderslot, stands on the right (east) bank of the Vecht River at its confluence with the IJsselmeer. As early as the beginning of the 10th century, a wooden tollhouse was erected on this site. Gradually it was rebuilt and enlarged. The castle, a red brick building, became a fortress after 1205 to guard the banks of the Vecht, and was reconstructed by Count Floris V of Holland who was assassinated here by noblemen in 1296. From 1621 the Muiderslot was the meeting place of a circle of poets and intellectuals led by P. C. Hooft (1581–1647), and brought together celebrities like Vondel, Grotius and Maria Tesselschade. This group became known as the Muiderkrinf. After Hooft's death, the castle was neglected, but in 1948 its interior was restored to the state of Hooft's day. A half hour spent exploring its galleries and enjoying the view of the IJsselmeer is well spent, especially in view of the fact that Holland has relatively few such relics of sterner times.

About 6 km. (4 miles) farther east is Naarden, a fortified town of 19,000 souls whose star-shaped ramparts and moats have been miraculously preserved despite a succession of bloody sieges and massacres. Here the dreaded Spanish Duke of Alva refined the art of torture; and here the French broke through in 1672. In comparison with other European walled cities it seems more like a toy fort, although observed from the air it shows correctness of design and stern obedience to the principles of self-protection. The 17th-century Bohemian pedagogue Comenius lived and died here (a special chapel perpetuates his memory) and the 1601 Dutch Renaissance Town Hall is charming inside. Thanks to outstanding acoustics, the 15th-century church is the locale for an annual performance of Bach's St. Matthew Passion.

Bussum, practically next door, wears a more modern aspect. So much so, in fact, that Holland's first television studios were established here amid the comfortable homes, wide boulevards, and public buildings.

Beyond Bussum we enter Gooiland, a region of lakes and woods whose scenic beauty has attracted the well-to-do from Amsterdam and elsewhere. Just 6 km. (4 miles) farther along is Laren, famous as an artists' colony. About the turn of the century, artists of the Hague School, attracted by the paintability of the district, congregated here and formed a group known as the luministen. Others joined them until today there are perhaps 200 modern painters and sculptors living in the neighborhood whose works are displayed from time to time in the Singer Memorial Foundation with its collection of paintings and engravings by the American artist William Singer, Jr.

Baarn (in the province of Utrecht), the other town of the wealthy, lies just south of the road we take to the costume towns of Bunschoten and Spakenburg, the latter with a fine IJsselmeer yachting harbor. The distinctive feature of the women's clothing here is the Kraplap, made of brightly flowered cotton, shaped like a cuirassier's breastplate and starched to about the same rigidity. The men's costumes have died out. The citizens have no religious scruples about being photographed.

Retracing our tracks to Baarn, we turn south with Soestdijk as our goal. A vaguely semicircular building by the side of the highway is the palace of the Queen Mother and Prince Bernhard, who may emerge with no fanfare in their own car.

Heading back towards Baarn a third time, we swing west along the Hilversum road, which runs past the Hooge Vuursche castle hotel.

Hilversum up the Vecht to Breukelen

Hilversum has two claims to distinction: it is the home of Dutch radio and TV broadcasting, and renowned for the outstanding modern architecture designed by Dudok. Although broadcasting is a state monopoly in the Netherlands with the government imposing a monthly license fee, the six stations are under Catholic, Protestant, Socialist, and independent management. Their studios, the schools, the public baths, and most particularly the angular Town Hall are among the outstanding examples of the architect's art.

Emerging on the west side of Hilversum we follow the road to Loenen, presently crossing the middle of the popular Loosdrecht Lakes, one of the most attractive swimming and yachting centers in the Netherlands. Loenen itself graces the west bank of the Vecht River, whose outlet into the IJsselmeer we saw during our visit to the castle at Muiden. The district from here south along the river to Breukelen and Maarssen enjoyed a great vogue during the second half of the 17th and the first half of the 18th century among prosperous Amsterdam merchants who built country houses beside the water in a style already showing signs of decadence, an abandonment of the austere classical line in favor of French influences. Many of these homes have been restored during recent years, and if the result is hardly Dutch, the effect is none the less delightful as the road winds and twists around each bend of the Vecht. These old patrician houses are best seen by taking a boat trip on the river.

We continue as far as Breukelen in the province of Utrecht, or possibly half a kilometer beyond to the 13th-century Castle of Nijenrode, on the right-hand side of the road, today a training school for Dutchmen planning to represent their companies abroad. Breukelen itself is just another sleepy town drowsing by the river bank, but

Americans may be startled to learn that it gave its name to Brooklyn, which still retains memories of the Dutch who founded it. On the water side of the village is the Breukelen bridge, rather more modest than its famous counterpart, since the river is no more than 6 meters (20 feet) wide at this point.

From Breukelen a 2-km. (1 mile) jog west brings us to the express highway that runs from Utrecht north to Amsterdam, a distance, from this point, of only 25 km. (16 miles). So enchanting is the Vecht district, however, that you may prefer to follow the river downstream to Loenen once again before turning west for the highway back to our starting point.

MOTORING AROUND THE IJSSELMEER

In addition, or as an alternative to the tours listed above, a circuit of the IJsselmeer is one of the most interesting trips you can make in Holland. You can start anywhere, of course, though Amsterdam will be a logical choice for many visitors, especially those who wish to rent a car for the purpose. A number of the places included on the itineraries mentioned below are described in this chapter, others in the chapters devoted to their respective regions.

Although it's possible to drive around the IJsselmeer in a single day, you are advised to allow at least two days for the journey. If you can spare three or four days, you can include one or two other stops en route.

Two-Day Itinerary

Amsterdam north to Volendam (brief pause), Edam (visit Kaasweg museum), Hoorn (visit De Waag or Weigh House in central square, also harbor), Enkhuizen (visit Zuiderzee Museum) for late lunch, then via Hoogkarspel and Wervershoof to Medemblik (brief pause) and Den Oever where the enclosing dike begins. In the middle, at Breezanddijk, is a monument with a tower that affords an outstanding view, where you can stop for tea or coffee. At the north end of the dike, turn south at Bolsward for Workum, Hindeloopen (pause for drive through town on the sea wall), Koudum (by-passing Staveren), Rijs, Oude Mirdum, Sondel, and Lemmer, where a fast road takes you across the Noordoostpolder to Emmeloord for a late dinner and the night.

In the morning, to Urk (best chance for parking is by the harbor) for costumes and a breath of the IJsselmeer, before continuing to Ens with a brief pause at Schokland to see the island and its minuscule museum. Continue southeast to Kampen, then swing southwest to Elburg (bypassing Zwolle) for an impression of its gridiron layout and almshouses. Nunspeet and Hierden are next; drive slowly for a glimpse of costumes, which are not so generally worn today. At Harderwijk, drive north along the dike as far as the Hardersluis pumping station (visit) for an impression of Holland's newest polder, then back to Harderwijk and on to the costume villages of Bunschoten and Spakenburg via Putten and Nijkerk. After a stop to sample Spakenburg, you return to Amsterdam by the main highway, detouring briefly at Naarden and Muiden.

This makes a very full two days and assumes an early start each morning.

Three-Day Itinerary

The first day is the same as the Two-Day Itinerary above, stopping overnight at Emmeloord.

In the morning you visit Urk and Schokland, as above, but instead of turning south at Ens you continue east to Vollenhove and St. Jansklooster, where you take the causeway across the delightful Beulaker Wijde to the crossroads De Blauwe Hand, turning left (north) from there for Giethoorn, the village that has canals and footpaths instead of streets. After a half-hour visit here, you continue east to Meppel, then swing south and turn off the main highway to drive through the costume villages of Staphorst (being sure not to take any pictures of the pious people who live there without their express permission) and Rouveen Zwolle is next (brief visit), followed by Elburg (visit as on Two-Day Itinerary) and Harderwijk, via Nunspeet and Hierden.

The trip out to Lelystad and a visit to its museum is interesting because of the impression you gain of what is involved in reclaiming land on so vast a scale.

The morning of the third day, cut east and slightly south to the villages of Lage Vuursche and Soestdijk for a glimpse of respectively Drakestein and Soestdijk palaces. Then swing over to Baarn and northwest through Laren to Naarden. Turn south once more to Hilversum, cut west across the pleasant Loosdrecht Lakes to Loenen, on the banks of the delightful Vecht River, lined with 17th-century country houses built by wealthy Amsterdammers. Turn south to Breukelen, which gave its name to New York City's famous borough.

From Breukelen follow the express highway back to Amsterdam if it's late in the day. If not, follow the Vecht River back to Loenen where, about 2 miles beyond, you can follow the east side of the Amsterdam-Rhine Canal north to Weesp and Muiden for a visit to Muiden Castle before returning to Amsterdam. Since the creation of the Bijlmermeer suburb of Amsterdam, the roads are gradually being rerouted, so follow the signposts carefully.

Four-Day Itinerary

This is an elaboration of the above. Allow yourself more time to explore Hoorn, Enkhuizen, and Medemblik, then cross the enclosing dike and spend the night in charming Sneek.

The next morning, head north for Leeuwarden (visit), west to Franeker (visit), then south to Bolsward, where the route into Emmeloord is the same as for the previous two itineraries.

The third and fourth days are the same as the second and third days of the Three-Day Itinerary.

In this tour you would be well advised to plan to spend an hour or so at the Dolphinarium at Harderwijk. This is an enthralling experience, because not only do the dolphins put up a remarkable circus performance but the directors also run a dolphin research station studying the special habits, and even the language, of these delightful creatures.

Not very far from Harderwijk is the Flevohof, a remarkable composite "working" exhibition of everything agricultural and horticultural in Holland. It gives the visitor, indeed, a day on a farm under unique conditions, with every form of visual display. And there is a host of fun entertainment for the children, water sports, etc.

Instead of returning to Amsterdam at the end of any of these tours, you can easily leave the shores of the IJsselmeer at Hilversum and turn south for Den Haag via either Utrecht, Woerden, Alphen a/d Rijn, and Leiden, or (more direct and much faster) Utrecht and thence by the express highway straight to Den Haag, preferably with a brief stop in Gouda.

PRACTICAL INFORMATION FOR THE
AMSTERDAM REGION

WHEN TO GO. As in the case of Amsterdam itself, the best time to visit its surroundings is from **May** to the end of **September,** with **July** and **August** being the peak months to avoid. Because of the bulbfields, the first week of May is possibly the best moment of all if flowers are high on your list of things to see. If spring comes early, however, the peak of the tulips, hyacinths, and narcissi can be as early as the middle of April, with nothing but heaps of discarded blooms left in the fields a fortnight later. The annual Bloemencorso or Flower Parade through the bulbfields takes place on the last Saturday in April, running from Haarlem to Lisse and back.

Because the bulbfields are such an unpredictable factor, they should not be given too much weight in the scheduling of your trip, especially if it is to be a brief one. There will still be plenty of flowers to see in May no matter what. Here are some of the other attractions:

The Keukenhof Gardens always open in late **March** nowadays and can be visited until approximately mid-May. The last Friday in **April** is the traditional beginning date of the sprightly Alkmaar cheese market, which continues every Friday morning until late **September.** *May 4* is Memorial Day. Haarlem is the site of the International Organ Competitions in early **July.** During the first two weeks in **August** international sailing regattas are staged at Loosdrecht, Muiden and Medemblik. In early **September,** Aalsmeer stages its annual flower parade, first at Aalsmeer, then at Amsterdam.

TELEPHONE CODES. We have given telephone codes for all the towns and villages in this chapter in the hotel and restaurant listings that follow. These codes need only be used when calling from outside the town or village concerned.

HOTELS AND RESTAURANTS. Because few tourists consider staying anywhere else but Amsterdam or Den Haag when they visit this corner of the Netherlands, hotel accommodations are relatively simple (with the notable exception of Hilversum). Moreover, most of the towns are so small that good restaurants are also scarce. If you are a little adventurous, however, and willing to put up with quarters that are spotlessly clean if basic, then there is no reason why you should feel bound to Amsterdam. Your reward will be a more leisurely pace through the countryside and the opportunity to come in closer contact with the Dutch themselves.

In many instances, the restaurant of the leading hotel may be the best place to stop for a meal. If so, no restaurant recommendations are made in the listing that follows. If you see *paling* (eel) on the menu, remember that it's often a specialty of the house. If you have your doubts, at least try the smoked variety as an appetizer on a piece of toast.

We have divided the hotels and restaurants in our listings into three categories—Expensive (E), Moderate (M) and Inexpensive (I). Most hotels, particularly at the upper end of the scale, have rooms in more than one category and a consequently wide range of prices. Remember, too, that many restaurants have dishes in more than one category, so be sure to check the menu outside *before* you go in. Look out too for the excellent-value Tourist Menu.

Figures in brackets after place names are mileage from Amsterdam.

ALKMAAR (22 northwest). Site of Holland's most interesting cheese market. *Alkmaar Comfort Inn* (M), 2 Arcadialaan; 072-120744. *Marktzicht* (M), 34 Houttil; 072–113283.

Restaurants. *t' Guiden Vlies* (M), 20 Koorstraat. *Kuiper* (M), 92 Spoorstraat. *Markzicht* (M), 34 Waagplein. *De Nachtegaal* (M), 100 Langestraat. *de Valkshoek* (M), offering really good food. *De Vriendschap* (M), 8 Schoolstraat.

BAARN (23 southwest). *De Hooge Vuursche* (E), 27 rooms with bath. Luxurious castle-hotel on the road to Hilversum; one of the best in the country. Extensive grounds, terraces, fountains, dancing. *De Prom* (M), 1 Amalialaan; 02154–12913. 40 rooms.

BENNEBROEK (14 southwest). **Restaurant.** *de Oude Geleerde Man* (M), 51 Rijksstraatweg. Highly recommended.

BERGEN (26 northwest). Once famous for its artists' colony. *Boschlust* (M), 60 Kruisweg; 02208–2060. 25 rooms. *Elzenhof* (M), 78 Doorpstraat; 02208–2401. 14 rooms, modest prices for quality. *Marijke* (M), 23 Dorpstraat (tel. 02208–2381). 45 rooms.

BERGEN AAN ZEE (3 west of Bergen). Quiet family seaside resort. *De Dennen* (E), 2 Parkweg. 25 rooms. *Nassau-Bergen* (E), 4 Van der Wyckplein; 02208–7541. 28 rooms, most with bath; near the beach. *De Stormvogel* (I), 12 Jac. Kalffweg; 02208–2734. 14 rooms.

BLOEMENDAAL (13 west). A garden suburb of Haarlem, 3 miles from the sea. *Iepenhove* (M); 023–258301. 62 rooms, some with bath. *Rusthoek* (M), 22 rooms, 10 with bath.

BOVENKARSPEL (67 northeast). **Restaurant.** *Roode Hert* (M), 235 Hoofstraat; 02285–11412. Romantically-housed in a 16th-century inn.

BUSSUM (16 east). On edge of the charming Gooiland district. *Gooiland* (M), 16 Stationsweg; 02159–43724. Small but comfortable.

Restaurants. *Auberge Maître Pierre* (E), 16 Stationsweg. On the pricey side, but worth it. *Warmolts* (E), 1–3 Nassaustraat. *Hotel Cecil* (M), 25 Brinklaan.

CALLANTSOOG (39 northwest). Small, seaside family resort. *De Wijde Blick* (M), 2 Zeeweg; 02248–1317. Small, with a good restaurant.

CASTRICUM (20 northwest). Quiet town on edge of the dunes, 3 miles from the beach. *Kornman* (M), 1 Mient; 02518–52251. 10 rooms, some with bath. **Restaurant.** *'t Eethuisje* (M), 53 Dorpsstraat.

DEN HELDER (48 north). Important naval base and ferry terminus for island of Texel. *Beatrix* (E), 2 Badhuisstraat; 02230–14800. 40 rooms, excellent. *Forest Hotel* (M), 10 rooms. *Motel den Helder* (M), 2 Marsdiepstraat; 02230–22333. 75 rooms.

DEN OEVER (45 north). Southern terminus of the enclosing dike that leads to Friesland. *Wiron* (M), 6 Zwinstraat; 02271–1404. *Zomerdijk* (M), 20 Voorstraat; 02271–1255.

EGMOND AAN ZEE (25 northwest). Seaside resort. *Bellevue* (M), A-7 Boulevard; 02206–1387. 50 rooms near the beach. *Frisia* (M), 24 rooms. *De Vergulde Valk* (I), 90 Voorstraat; 02206–1291. 10 rooms, few with bath.

EDAM (14 northeast). *Damhotel* (M), 1 Keizersgracht. *Fortune* (M), 5 Spuistraat.

ENKHUIZEN (35 northeast). Attractive old walled city. *Het Wapen van Enkhuizen* (E), 59 Breedstraat; 02280–13434. Not all rooms with bath. *Die Port van Cleve* (M), 74 Dijk; 02280–12510. 20 rooms, near the sea.

Restaurant. *Koffieshop/Restaurant Alpino* (M), 120a Westerstraat.

HAARLEM (12 west). *Lion d'Or* (E), 34 Kruisweg; 023–321750. 80 beds. *Die Raeckse* (M), 1 Raaks; 023–326629. 35 rooms.

Restaurants. *Dreezicht* (M), in the woods. *Lantaern* (M), with an Old Dutch interior. *Los Gauchos* (M), 9 Kruisstraat.

HILVERSUM (20 southeast). *Het Hof van Holland* (E), 1 Kerksbrink; 035–46141. 30 rooms with bath. *Hilvertsom* (M), 28 Koninginneweg; 035–232444. 44 rooms, some with bath.

Restaurants. *Het Zwarte Paard* (M), la Larenseweg. *Me Chow Low* (M), 25 Groest. *Palace Residence* (M), 86 s' Gravelandseweg. *Rôtisserie Napoléon* (M), in the Hotel de Nederlanden at nearby Vreeland. A local favorite.

HOORN (25 north). Historic seaport. *Petit Noord* (M), 55 Kleine Noord; 02290–12750. 34 rooms, all with bath; pleasant restaurant.

Restaurants. *De Waag* (M), 8 Roode Steen; 02290–15195. Historical restaurant situated in a 17th-century weigh-house. *Petit-Restaurant Marcelly* (M), 25 Lange Kerkstraat.

IJMUIDEN (16 northwest). Gateway to the North Sea Canal. *Royal* (M), 93 Kennemerlaan; 02550–12743.

KATWOUDE, near Volendam (see below). *Katwoude Motel* (M), 1 Wagenweg; 02993–65656. 30 rooms.

LAREN (18 southeast). Artists' colony just outside Hilversum. *De Witte Bergen* (E), 50 rooms with shower. *Herberg t'Langenbaergh* (M), 1 Deventerweg; 05783–1209. 7 rooms.

Restaurant. *Le Postillon de la Provence* (E), 2 Westherheide; 035–87974. Excellent French restaurant with superb sea food.

MAARSSEN (10 southeast). *De Nonnerie* (M), 51 Lange Gracht; 03465–62201. 10 rooms.

Restaurant. *Wilgenplas* (M); excellent food.

MEDEMBLIK (64 north). *Het Wapen van Medemblik* (M), 1 Oosterhaven; 02274–3844. 28 rooms; good quality for the price.

Restaurant. *Twee Schouwtjes* (M), 27 Oosterhaven; 02274–1956. Good restaurant in 16th-century house.

OUDERKERK (4 south). Sleepy village on the Amstel river. *t'Jagerhuis* (M), 4 Amstelzijde; 02963–1432. 25 rooms; closed Dec.

Restaurant. *de Paardenburg* (E), 55 Amstelzijde. One of the region's best.

SASSENHEIM (10 south of Haarlem). *Motel Sassenheim* (M), 8 Warmonderweg; 02522–19019. 30 rooms with bath; recommended.

SCHAGEN (38 northwest). *de Roode Leeuw* (M), 15 Markt; 02240–12537. 24 beds, 2 rooms with bath.

TEXEL ISLAND (60 north). Reached by ferry from Den Helder; most hotels close during the winter. At **De Koog**, on Texel's west shore: *Het Gouden Boltje* (M), 44 Dorpstraat; 02228–755. 15 rooms; closed Nov.–Dec. *Opduin* (E), 42 rooms with bath. *Prinses Juliana* (E), 22 Ruyslaan; 02228–445. 46 rooms with bath. *Het Gouden Boltje* (M), 44 Dorpstraat; 02228–755. 15 rooms; closed Nov.–Dec.

Restaurant. *Tubantia* (M), 133 Pontweg.

At **Den Burg**, the island's capital: *den Burg* (M), 2 Emmalaan; 02220–2106. 18 rooms.

Restaurants. *De Lindeboom* (M), 14 Groeneplaats. *De Raadskelder* (M), 6 Vismarkt.

VELSEN (18 northwest). **Restaurant.** *Taveerne Beeckestijn,* 136 Rijksweg; 02550–14469. Located in an annex of Huis Beekestijn, an 18th-century mansion with period rooms.

VOLENDAM (14 northeast). *Spaander* (M), 15 Haven; 02993–16359. 40 rooms. *Van Diepen* (M), 35 Haven; 02993–63705.

WIJK AAN ZEE (17 northwest). Quiet seaside resort. *De Klughte* (M), 2 Van Ogtropweg; 02517–4304. 20 rooms. *Het Hoge Duin* (M), 50 Rijkert Aertsweg; 02517–5943. 27 rooms, all with shower. Situated on the dunes, 130 feet above sea level; restaurant has good sea food. *Welgelegen* (I), 2 De Zwaanstraat; 02517–4323. No bathrooms attached.

Restaurant. *Sonnevanck* (M), 2 Rijckert Aertsweg.

ZANDVOORT AAN ZEE (18 west). Popular North Sea resort. *Bouwes Palace* (E), 7 Badhuisplein; 02507–15041. 60 rooms, all with bath; also, self-service apartments. *Bouwes* (E), 44 rooms with bath; broad terraces, casino, dancing, nightclub, dolphinarium. *Hoogland* (E), 5 Westerpovkstraat; 02507–15541. 25 rooms. *Astoria* (M), 155 Dr. C.A. Gerkestraat; 02507–14550. 18 rooms, all with bath. *van Petegem,* 86 Haarlemerstraat; 02707–2076. 10 rooms, none with baths.

Restaurants. *Castell Plage* (M), summer-only restaurant in beach pavilion. *Duivenvoorden* (M), 49 Haltestraat. *Harocamo* (M), 14 Kerkstraat. *Stella Maris* (M), 1 Strandweg. *De Uitzichttoren* (M), in the top of the 200-ft. tower that dominates the town; offers a remarkable view even if the food is so-so.

GETTING AROUND. By Car. This is the best way of all for seeing this part of Holland. Distances are short, there are no big cities outside of Haarlem and Hilversum, and you can return to Amsterdam for the night after each excursion, if you wish. If you do drive, buy one of the detailed maps published by the ANWB motoring organization (offices at 5 Museumplein in Amsterdam, or 117A Schotersingel in Haarlem). This will enable you to leave main roads and explore the delightful byways of the region in complete confidence that you can always find your way back at the end of the day by the most direct route. Almost every corner of this country is a delight, even the remote lanes being paved, so avoid the highway whenever you can.

A point to remember, whatever your means of transportation, is that nearly every city and town mentioned in this chapter can be visited from Den Haag with almost as much ease as from Amsterdam, thanks to the compact nature of this angle of the Netherlands. You might consider, therefore, visiting everything north of Amsterdam (excursions 1 and 2: see text) from that city and then doing the rest from Den Haag or Utrecht, so as to have a little variety.

By Train. All the key towns in this area can be reached conveniently by train. On Friday mornings in July and August there is a special 'Cheese Express' that leaves the Central Station in Amsterdam about 9:40 A.M., arriving in Alkmaar about 10:15, in time for the market. Haarlem is also easily reached by trains that leave the Central Station roughly every half hour. The trip takes about 15 minutes.

Excursions. A wide variety of inclusive sightseeing tours from Amsterdam are available. Among the many on offer are: a 3-hour bus and boat tour covering Monnickendam, Marken and Volendam, cost is around Fl. 35; an 8-hour tour around the Zuiderzee covering Urk, Hindeloopen, Makkum and Hoorn, cost is around Fl. 50. Most of these tours are by bus and start from the area around the Central Station in Amsterdam, but there are also special inclusive day excursions organized by the national railway. Details of these and all other tours are available from the VVV in Amsterdam in the Central Station.

There is also an interesting boat excursion from Harderwijk, which leaves every hour during the summer and lasts about 70 minutes. The trip covers Veluwemeer and the polder reclamation work in progress.

TOURIST INFORMATION. There are regional VVV offices at the following places: **Aalsmeer,** 8 Stationsweg (tel. 02977–25374); **Alkmaar,** 3 Waagplein (tel. 072–114284); **Bussum,** 6 Wilhelminaplantsoen (02159–30264); **Haarlem,** 1 Stationsplein (tel. 023–319059); **Hilversum,** 21 Stationsplein (tel. 035–11651); **Hoorn,** in the Weigh House on the main square (tel. 02290–18193); **Texel,** 9 Groenplaats, Den Burg (tel. 02220–4741).

MUSEUMS. Among the many local museums that deal with the history of various towns in this region, there are a number of more than passing interest to the visitor from abroad. Some have been discussed in detail in the text, but it is useful to list them alphabetically.

ALKMAAR. Stedelijk Museum (Municipal Museum), in the Town Hall. Details facets of the town's development, especially the siege by the Spanish in 1573, which was successfully resisted.

BERGEN. Het Sterkenhuis, Oude Prinseweg. Small museum in house dating from 1655. Has interesting exhibits on the defeat, at Bergen, in 1799 of the Duke of York's British and Russian army by the French.

EDAM. Captain's House, Damplein (opposite Town Hall). Fascinating museum showing how a retired sea captain lived in the 18th century. Richly furnished with period items, plus a cellar that literally floats.

Kaaswag (Cheese Weigh House). In a building dating from 1823; interesting exhibitions on cheese. Open Apr.–end Sept. only.

ENKHUIZEN. Stedelijk Waagmuseum, Kaasmarkt. Located in the old weight house; also, interesting exhibitions of contemporary art in the attic.

Wapenmuseum, located in the old prison; good collections of arms and armor through the ages.

Zuiderzee Buitenmuseum. Open-air museum, opened only in 1983; attractive and carefully-reconstructed old buildings, including a church, from around the Zuiderzee. Open Apr.–end Sept. Adm. Fl. 7.50.

Zuiderzee Museum, in the Peperhuis. Located in what was once a ware house belonging to the East Indies Company, the museum has good exhibits on many aspects of life in the Zuiderzee; fishing, costumes and furniture etc.

HAARLEM. Frans Hals Museum. Groot Helig Land. In early 17th-century almshouse, contains marvelous collection of pictures by Hals, plus some by contemporaries. In summer, candlelit concerts are held here.

Teylers Museum, 16 Spaarne. The oldest museum in the country, established by wealthy merchant in 1778 as museum of science and arts. Has a number of drawings by Michelangelo and Raphael.

DEN HELDERS. Helders Marinemuseum (Maritime Museum). Located in attractive building dating from 1820s; traces the history of the Dutch Royal Navy since 1813.

HOORN. Westfries Museum, Rode Steen. Located in beautiful building dating from 1632; museum traces the development of the town, especially the exploration and colonization of the Far East, in which Hoorn played a leading role.

KOOG AAN DER ZAAN. Molenmuseum (Windmill Museum). 18 Museumlaan. History of the windmill in Holland; models, pictures etc.

LAREN. Singer Museum, 1 Oude Drift. Works of William Henry Singer Jr.; paintings of the American, French and Dutch schools, plus changing exhibitions.

LELYSTAD. Informatiecentrum Nieuw Land. Fascinating and excellently displayed museum tracing the draining and reclamation of areas around the IJsselmeer and the building of the modern town of Lelystad.

LIMMEN. Bulb Museum, 81 Dusseldorperweg. Survey of bulb farming in Holland during the past 200 years.

MUIDEN. Muiderslot. 13th-century moated castle; fascinating both inside and out. A tavern in the wine cellar is open from mid-May to the end of August.

NAARDEN. Vesting Museum (Fortification Museum), Westwalstraat. Underground and open-air museum with casemates, cannon-cellar and collection of historical objects.

VIJFHUIZEN. Museum de Cruquius, 23 Cruquiusdijk. Housed in historic polder pumping station built in 1849, museum provides exce¹lent coverage of the country's battle against the sea and the draining of polders. Good models of windmills etc.

DE ZAANSE SCHANS. Open-air collections of Zaan wood sculptures, houses and windmills. Open summer only.

SHOPPING. Cheese is the great specialty throughout this area. It's best bought at the various colorful markets that most towns hold. All the most popular places also have shops selling the full range of the country's crafts industry. For bulb lovers, Lisse is the place to head for. Special arrangements can be made for sending bulbs home (direct importation is not generally allowed).

Moving upmarket, Haarlem is renowned for its antique shops, with prices generally lower than in Amsterdam or Den Haag.

SHOPPING

From Diamonds and Delft to Cheese and Cigars

The question of what to take home as a souvenir of the Netherlands has as many facets as one of the glittering Amsterdam diamonds. If your purse and luggage are limited, you can always tuck a piece of pewter into your suitcase, or an antique *koekeplank* (cookie mould) carved with amusing designs. Other possibilities in the same category include pretty enamel ashtrays, blue-and-white Delftware, crystal from Leerdam or Maastricht, a Gouda cheese, or a box of those delicious hard candies called *Haagse Hopjes*.

Amsterdam is the logical place to start for most tourists, although Den Haag, thanks to the presence of the diplomatic colony as well as the European headquarters of many international companies, can offer almost as wide and varied a selection. Venturing farther afield, Haarlem, Delft, Leiden, and in fact, almost every town can also be interesting, as they frequently have more "local" antiques at prices lower than in the large cities. It is astonishing to see the wealth of antique treasures still in Holland, and although some of these come from other countries, many of them are genuinely Dutch, while the remainder can almost always be relied on to be authentic articles from elsewhere. The shops tend to be localized in particular streets or districts, making it easy to shop-hop.

Further, many places like Den Haag or Breda, for example, have antique markets in the town center during summer. These are generally supervised by the local authorities, although of course, no guarantee is given about authenticity. Still, many a good bargain, Dutch and foreign, can be picked up in these marketplaces. Prices are usually reasonable and a little bargaining occasionally makes them more so. Details of the locations of these markets will be found under the Practical Information sections at the end of each regional chapter.

Amsterdam, Home of the Diamond Cutters

During the Middle Ages, Antwerp was Europe's great diamond center. After the Spanish conquest of 1576, many diamond experts fled north to Amsterdam. During the latter part of the 17th century, master gem-cutters from persecuted religious groups all over the Continent found refuge in Amsterdam. This, timed with the discovery of Brazilian diamond fields, gave the industry a tremendous boost. At the French court of Louis XV, brilliants were in high demand to set off powdered wigs. In those days, facets were made by rubbing two diamonds together on a wheel turned by women. Violent protest was voiced by the fairer sex in 1822 when horse-power began replacing feminine hands. At that time, when a shipload of raw diamonds arrived from India or Brazil, there was feverish activity for several months until the cargo was cut and the finished stones sent, with Paris the principal destination, to be sold. Then factories stood idle until a new shipment landed.

Political upheavals throughout Europe during the latter part of the 19th century caused a serious crisis in the diamond industry. Unexpectedly, it was saved by children of a Dutch farmer living near Hopetown, South Africa, who discovered that the pebbles in a nearby stream made marvelous toys. For 500 sheep, 10 oxen, and one horse, one of these twinkling marbles representing 21 carats, found its way to Europe. The diamond rush was on and Kimberley, South Africa, became the big center. In 1870, the first shipment of South African diamonds reached Europe, commencing a trade that today supplies 90 per cent of the world's diamonds.

A visit to one of the modern diamond centers in Amsterdam offers the visitor a brief education in this fascinating business. You will see a demonstration with glass dummies which shows how the diamond is mined, cut, and polished. It is a process which fascinatingly combines modern techniques with the kind of skill only learned through many generations of craftsmen. First, each diamond is examined by experts to determine its exact color, weight, grain, and possible flaws. Then it is decided how it should be cut. Later, the finished product is scrutinized for quality and price. One of the great triumphs of the diamond cutter's art was the work on the world's largest diamond (the Cullinan), which represented over 3,000 carats when it was discoverd in Transvaal in 1905 and presented to King Edward VII of England. After months of study, the fabulous stone was split to make the world's largest polished diamond. It was set in the crown of England. Another massive gem from the same stone was placed in the royal scepter and two more have been mounted in a pin for Queen Elizabeth II. The smallest in the world was also cut here as a demonstration of master technique. It weighed ¼ of a milligram; or 1/2,500,000 of the Cullinan.

We are told that it takes an entire day to saw one carat. Next comes the cleaving or shaping by hand, followed by the important polishing process, which gives the diamond its 58 different facets. You will notice that the size of a gem is usually proportionate to the number of grey hairs on the head of its worker, for it takes 15 years of experience to know how to polish the big stuff. The untrained eye can tell a good diamond at one glance by its blue-white color. You could do worse than to choose a sparkling diamond as a life-long souvenir of your visit to Holland—it will cost considerably less than elsewhere. There is also an excellent diamond store in the duty-free Shopping Center at Schiphol Airport.

Solid Dutch Silver

Silver is considered to be another good buy in Holland. The metallic content of its products is guaranteed by special controlling marks. The marks consist of a lion and number, indicating the purity of the silver, either .925 (sterling quality) or the more usual .833, to which may be added the town and markers marks. Much antique silver was also stamped with the coat of arms of the city of its origin and sometimes the guild mark of its maker.

For example, three crosses topped by a crown was the mark of old Amsterdam, while a stork was the mark used by silversmiths in Den Haag. Indeed by law all Dutch silver must be hallmarked, which makes buying modern silver much easier, but the knowledge of marks on old pieces is a specialized business and one that should be researched very carefully; otherwise, it's best to buy from a reputable dealer, who will explain, and should guarantee, its origin.

A number of museums, large and small, feature collections of fine old silver. Notable are the display in Amsterdam's Rijksmuseum and in the Friesland museum in Leeuwarden.

The Dutch silver industry in Voorschoten started about 100 years ago in a small shed. It is now known as Van Kempen & Begeer and an enlarged factory stands there on this firm's private property. For silver filigree work and embossed plaques, the Dutch government has set up a school for the cultivation of fine silversmiths and goldsmiths in Schoonhoven.

In recent years a large trade has been built up in Holland in English and Continental silver, especially tea and coffee services, candelabra, and Victorian and Georgian tableware. Prices are admittedly high, but for visitors to Europe who cannot include a trip to England in their itinerary, this sort of souvenir can often be a good buy. All the large Dutch jewellers' shops carry extensive stocks of this old silver.

When looking for not too expensive jewellery as souvenirs, ask to be shown rings, bracelets or brooches and tie-pins with the traditional *Zeeuwse knop* or Zeeland knob pattern: a silver filigree rosette. They make an unusual and original gift and are not very painful to your purse.

Delve into Delft

Most gift counters, hotel lobbies, and china shops are littered with so-called Delftware, much of it mass produced by factories in Gouda. The art of making the authentic blue-and-white earthenware, however, is not extinct.

In the 17th century, 30 different potteries produced Delft china. Now there are only two, of which the Royal Factory at Delft is the most famous. Founded in 1653, it bears the worthy name of De Porceleyne Fles. On the bottom of each object that is produced a triple signature appears: a plump vase topped by a straight line, the stylized letter *F* below it, and the word Delft. The only discernible difference between a new piece of hand-painted Delft and an old one is age. Genuine Delft may be recognized by its color, the fine shine of its glaze, the complexity of its design, and the superlative way it is expressed. The varying shades of blue found in Delft depend on the particular artist. Small scattered leaves known as the parsley pattern are characteristic of many of its pieces. The big floral splotches or simple portraits without detail are usually produced by practicing beginners.

The price of a genuine Delft article is never determined by its size but by the quality of its painting. As every object is hand-drawn, unaided by stencils or tracings, the quantity is exceedingly limited. You can understand that an entire Delft dinner service is rare; it becomes too expensive for the buyer as well as an interminable bore for the artist to complete. On weekdays visitors are welcome at De Porceleyne Fles in Delft (Rotterdamseweg 196) to see its showroom of exquisite museum pieces as well as demonstrations with the potters' wheel, the oven, and the brush. Although blue and white Delft sprinkled with floral bouquets is the most popular, other variations of Delftware do exist.

The milk-white ware, without design, was exclusively for kitchen use during the 17th century. However, in 1936 a small white collection of ridged, petal-edged decorative pieces was started, using the old moulds. Recently, a new line of white has been introduced, featuring sleek smooth forms to suit modern interiors. Also keeping step with the present is an entirely original conception of Delft that alternates black with earthy tones of gray and brown in unusual futuristic shapes, decorated by Wynblad-inspired etchings of people scratched into the glaze, rather than painted below it.

In 1948, a rich red cracked glaze was introduced depicting profuse flowers, graceful birds, and leaping gazelles. (The special cracked texture of this pottery is achieved only after six or seven bakings.) A range of green, gold, and black known as New-Delft is exquisitely drawn with minuscule figures to resemble an old Persian tapestry.

The marvelous Pynacker Delft borrowing Japanese motifs dominated by rich orange with gold, deep blue, and touches of green, has existed since the 17th century. The brighter Polychrome Delft carries a bolder picture in sun-flower yellow, vivid orange, and blue with green suggestions.

Magnificent reproductions of canvases made by 17th-century artists are executed on circular dishes in blue or brown sepia. For a goodish price, you can have your portrait drawn on a Delft plate. De Porceleyne Fles even produces a limited number of unpainted, specially glazed tiles for industrial uses in buildings, bathrooms, and swimming pools.

A commemorative tile or wall-plate could well provide that "different" present. Of the many designs for a new baby, there is one with the child's name, place, and date of birth encircling a grandfather clock, denoting the hour and the minute, and a cradle. Dutch *jenever* and liqueurs, too, bottled in blue-and-white Delftware jugs or Gouda china dolls in national costume make attractive gifts. These items, of course, along with many of the so-called Delft tiles, are found everywhere in souvenir shops, and are seldom made in Delft.

There are, indeed, several Dutch makes of pottery which make good souvenirs. Some have much the same design and color as Delft and are usually somewhat cheaper, while others have their own distinctive designs. The name of the maker is always given on the bottom of the piece, so there is no risk of mistaking it for Delft or any make of English or Continental pottery. In addition to the better known Delft wares, attractive traditional and folk designs of pottery are found in some of the smaller towns, such as Makkum and Warkum, in Friesland.

Pewter Pots and Plates, Crystal

During the 17th century, pewter was a necessary complement to Delft blue plates. However, age is no guarantee that the pewter you unearth in an antique shop is fine. 300 years ago, they made bad pewter just as they do today. Cast in old moulds, Meeuws' handwrought pewter tends to retain the original shapes you see pictured in the museums. Pewter is a mixture of tin and lead. The greater lead content a piece contains, the more worthless it becomes . . . bending easily, tarnishing quickly, and denting without apparent cause. Don't be misled by the bright appearance of those long necked jugs you see in the knicknack shops around town. Look for the heavy duty quality, preferably Meeuws' if it is new, with only five percent lead and an eternal shine.

Leerdam crystal has become famous for its fine design and lovely blue-white color. The forms vary from wide-mouthed champagne glasses balanced on cut stems to generous cornucopian vases to elegant glittery candlesticks to chubby beer beakers. Ask any reliable glass shop to let you see a complete catalogue of stocks and styles. Maastricht crystal, though as beautiful as Leerdam, is generally less expensive. Heavier, more cut, and worked, it often resembles the French Baccarat while its competitor to the north can be compared to Swedish Orrefors.

Dutch cigars are always a good buy as gifts, but bear in mind your Customs quota.

If you do not want to carry cheeses home with you, you might find that cheese accessories such as cutting boards with small glass domes, or specially designed knives, make very acceptable souvenirs.

When you want to take home a pair of clogs, do NOT buy them at a souvenir shop but ask for them when in the country, where the farmers buy them. You'll get them for a much lower price and there will be more choice.

Eatables, Drinkables and Plantables

The Dutch love to eat and drink and their favorite foods provide splendid opportunities for souvenir and gift shopping. Dutch cheeses and the potent *jenever* gin are obvious choices, but Holland also produces a wide range of liqueurs such as *Curaçao,* or *Advocaat,* a type of egg nog, and many flavored with fruit or herbs. Dutch chocolate and a variety of specialized candies cater for those with a sweet tooth, while pickled herring, or smoked eel, are delicious savoury souvenirs.

The bulbfields of Holland are among the country's top scenic attractions and their products are ideal as gifts to take home. One word of warning, here, on the regulations applied by some countries to imports of plants, which may limit the type or quantity of such produce that can be taken home, but commercial growers offering plants or bulbs for sale can advise on these regulations for most countries and will supply appropriate purchases.

A Last Word

If you are leaving the Netherlands by air it might be useful to remember that the tax-free shops at both Schiphol (Amsterdam) and Rotterdam Airports, open for long hours, offer a mouth-watering display of cameras, watches, liquors, tobacco, perfume, jewelry, toys, porcelain, and the flower bulbs and seed for which Holland is so justly famous, at prices which are often lower than in the ordinary shops. Since the standard of duty-free shops around the world is so variable, many of them being far more expensive than the stores just around the corner from you at home, it is a pleasure to be able to record that Schiphol at least is full of genuine bargains.

DUTCH FOOD AND DRINK

Homelike or Exotic—Always Hearty

Her sons and daughters having ranged the four corners of the earth
for several centuries, Holland can offer you a large variety of cooking,
while the frequent trips which Dutch businessmen make abroad have
served to ensure that the foreign cuisine in Holland, when it is good,
is very, very good. If your soul yearns for them, and your pocket-book
can stand the strain, *Cole Cardinale, Steak Orloff,* and *Canard à l'O-
range* are yours for the ordering.

But real Dutch cooking is made of sterner stuff. Simple, solid nour-
ishment, without any fancy trimmings that might hide the basic high
quality of the food, is what warms the cockles of the average Dutchman's culinary heart. As a result, Dutch cooking is often called unimaginative. This is only relatively true. An abundant variety of meat,
fish and fowl, vegetables and fruit, at reasonable prices, do not oblige

the Dutch cook to resort to ingenuity when preparing a meal. The true Dutch cook is inclined to be lavish with butter and the result is often a strain on the digestive systems of those used to lighter fare.

At the other extreme, Indonesian food, with its variety of spices and exotic dishes, provides a dramatic contrast to the blander Dutch fare. But in between nowadays, almost every large town has a wide range of restaurants specializing in their own brands of 'national' dishes, running from Chinese to Italian, French to Yugoslavian, and even American to English. Your hotel porter will tell you where to go for any particular kind of food, while most of the local tourist offices (VVV) have restaurant lists which will help you to solve your eating problems.

When to Eat

The mealtime pattern is remarkably uniform throughout Holland. Breakfast is customarily served either in your room or in the hotel's dining room. It invariably consists of several varieties of bread and rolls, thin slices of Dutch cheese, prepared meats and sausage, butter and jam or honey, often a boiled egg, and a pot of steaming coffee, tea, or chocolate. Fruit juices are generally available but not cheap.

Don't be astonished if the waiter presents you with your hotel bill when you have finished breakfast (assuming you are preparing to leave). This custom, especially prevalent at provincial hotels, is actually a convenience and saves you the trouble of having to settle up at the last minute.

The typical lunch is *koffietafel,* which consists of more bread, various cold cuts, cheese and conserves. There is usually a side dish—warm (an omelette, a small individual cottage pie, or the like) or cold (a salad, Russian eggs, or something similar)—to go with it. The whole is washed down with tea or coffee.

The evening meal is usually the major repast of the day and is often eaten quite early—6 P.M. to 6.30 P.M.

Coffee at 11 in the morning (or earlier) and tea at 4 in the afternoon are equally sacred rituals.

What to Eat

Tradition has its place in Dutch eating. Although many dishes which were a part of the Dutch way of life before the advent of heated glasshouses, canning, deep-freeze, and modern transport facilities are now no longer a necessity, people still relish them.

To start with soup, there are two which can be called typically Dutch. *Erwtensoep*—a thick pea soup, usually only available October through March. Often served with pieces of smoked sausage, cubes of pork fat, pig's knuckle, and slices of brown or white bread. The other is *Groentensoep*—a clear consommé, loaded with vegetables, vermicelli, and tiny meatballs.

Hutspot—a hotchpotch of potatoes, carrots and onions with a historical background. When the siege of Leiden was raised on October 3rd, 1574, the starving populace was given, first, salted herring and white bread, then *hutspot* with *klapstuk* (stewed lean beef of which a little goes a long way). This has become such a traditional dish that you will find Dutchmen eating it on October 3rd anywhere from the North Pole to the Equator, from New York to Hong Kong.

Herring—eaten all the year round, the Dutch delight in the salted variety, but especially in "green herring" (those caught during the first three weeks of the fishing season which starts in May). You can eat herring neatly filleted and served on toast as an hors d'oeuvre in any restaurant, but half the fun is buying it from a pushcart, holding the herring by the tail, and gobbling it down like a native. The first cask of new herring is traditionally presented to the Queen.

Rolpens met Rodekool—thin slices of spiced and pickled minced beef and tripe, sautéed in butter, topped with a slice of apple, and served with red cabbage.

Boerenkool met Rookworst—a hotchpotch of frost-crisped kale and potatoes, served with smoked sausage.

Zuurkool—Sauerkraut: "garni" means with streaky bacon, gammon, and sausage.

Stokvis—an old-time favorite few restaurants serve nowadays. If you'd like to try something really different this is your dish. The basis is dried whitefish, cooked in milk and drained, served with potatoes and rice, fried onions, sliced raw onions, chopped dill pickles, melted butter and mustard sauce.

Kapucijners—Marrowfat peas, served with boiled potatoes, chunky pieces of stewed beef, fried bacon cubes, french fried onions, slivers of raw onion, dill pickles, mustard pickles, melted butter, molasses, and a green salad. Believe it or not the result is delicious.

Remember that nearly all the above dishes, like so many traditional dishes in Europe, are winter fare.

Seafood—fish of all kinds is usually well prepared in Holland. Try, for example, *gebakken zeetong* (fried sole) or *lekkerbekjes*—specially prepared fried whiting. Royal imperial oysters, mainly from Zeeland, are still an epicurean dish, while the smaller equally tasty "petites" are also good. Both types, however, are expensive. Dutch shrimps taste much better than they look. If your purse is well filled, try lobster (but ask the price first), as this is a real luxury. Crab is rarely available. Mussels, on the other hand, are cheap and if you love them there's always a fish restaurant somewhere around, or buy them, fried in batter, from a fishmonger. Eel is plentiful. Smoked, filleted, and served on buttered toast, it has a bouquet and flavor that is more easily praised than described; the smaller-sized eels taste better than the large ones. In this form it normally serves as an hors d'oeuvre. It is also eaten stewed or fried (but again, ask the price first).

Dessert—Here the Dutch, on the whole, do not shine and generally rely on ice-cream or fruit with lashings of whipped cream to carry the day. Dutch pancakes *(flensjes* or *pannekoeken)* in all their 25 varieties are good. To mention but one, which is a meal in itself, *spekpannekoek,* is a pancake measuring about a foot across, and about half an inch thick. It should be loaded with bits of crisp, streaky bacon and be full of air pockets. It is served with apple syrup or molasses. Three other favorites are *wafels met slagroom* (waffles with whipped cream), *poffertjes,* which can only be described as small lumps of dough, fried in butter and dusted with powdered sugar, but which the Dutch insist taste "as if an angel had caressed your tongue", and *spekkoek*—which literally means "bacon cake", probably because it looks like best-quality streaky bacon. The recipe comes from Indonesia and it consists of alternate layers of heavy butter sponge and spices. It tastes delicious and, besides fruit, is the only congruous dessert to a *rijsttafel.*

Snacks—Nearly every town in Holland has many snack bars. Here you can get a *broodje* (roll) or sandwich in a hurry. These come in an infinite variety ranging from plain cheese to what amounts to a modest *hors d'oeuvre.* One of Holland's favorites is the *uitsmijter.* This is an open-face sandwich consisting of two fried eggs, laid on a foundation of ham, roast beef or cheese, on slices of buttered bread; potato and meat croquettes have recently become great favorites. The snack bars also offer several kinds of soup, cake, pastry, and ice-cream and some have a menu with two or three *plats du jour,* and an "A" license, which means that besides tea, coffee, and soft drinks they can also sell beer and wines. The service is usually fast and the cost modest.

What to Drink

Like the kitchen, Dutch bars are for the most part internationally-minded. First-class hotels and top restaurants in major cities have learned to make good martinis and similar cocktails. The indigenous drink, of course, is gin or *jenever,* a colorless, potent beverage that is served chilled, or at room temperature, in shot glasses and should be drunk neat as it does not mix well with any other liquid. Some Dutchmen drink it with cola or vermouth—but unless you have a very strong head avoid deviations. It comes in many varieties depending on the spices used, if any. *Jonge,* or young jenever, contains less sugar, is less creamy, but no less intoxicating than *oude,* or old, jenever. The *Bols* brand, still available in the famous stone crock which, when emptied of its original contents, was often used as a hot water bottle in wintertime, is best-known to most tourists, whereas the Dutch often prefer *Bokma,* although *De Kuyper* and *Claeryn* are also favored brands. If you don't like your gin straight try a *kleine angst* (literally little terror), which is a shot of young jenever with a liberal dash of angostura bitters. Don't gulp your jenever as the Dutch do—remember they're used to it! This innocuous, mild-tasting liquid has a delayed action which might have unfortunate results.

If you don't feel up to the challenge of tasting the Dutch water of life, they have an infinite choice. Besides the many kinds of sherry, vermouth, port and various beverages available in other countries, Holland offers a long list of gins—*bessen-jenever* (red-current gin), *citroen-jenever* (lemon gin), and so forth, as well as *advocaat* (a heavier and creamier variety of egg-nog).

Many Dutchmen drink beer with their meals. You'll make no mistake if you follow their example, because Dutch beer is good, always properly cooled and inexpensive. Imported Danish, English, Belgian and German beer is usually available, at about twice the price. Unless you want one of the heavier varieties just ask for a *pils.*

Better restaurants and hotel dining rooms will nearly always offer you a wine list. If you find the vintage you particularly fancy and don't mind the cost, order away. But unless you have a particular interest in wine, stick to beer or water (which may have to be asked for).

Many restaurants nowadays serve a carafe or individual glasses of *vins du pays* which is both palatable and reasonable. But where the wine lists are concerned the wines are generally good and with a wide range, and in comparison with other countries cannot be called expensive, except at the luxury hotels and restaurants.

Dutch liquers, on the other hand, are excellent and reasonable. *Curaçao* takes its name from the island of the same name in the Dutch West Indies. It receives its flavor from the peel of a special variety of orange grown there and is delicious. *Triple Sec* is almost the same thing as Cointreau, though a shade less subtle. *Parfait d'Amour* is a highly perfumed, amethyst-colored liqueur. Dutch-made versions of crême de menthe, apricot brandy, anisette, and similar liqueurs are also very good.

Brand name whiskies from Scotland, Canada and the United States are on sale at prices below those charged at home. But the Dutch produce several quite potable bottled whiskies, as well as several varieties of passable dry gin suitable for nearly all mixed drinks.

Indonesian Cooking

Although Indonesian food tastes good at any time of the day, your digestion will probably appreciate it if you stick to lunch. The best restaurants are in Den Haag, Amsterdam and Rotterdam, although nearly all towns now have good ones. Generally, however, they are nowadays announced as Indonesian-Chinese places, and both types of food are always available. But it is always a good idea to have a chat with the manager, or the waiter, to get an explanation of what the dishes are composed of. This is particularly the case with the Chinese food, although most menu cards have English translations.

The most elaborate Indonesian meal is called a *rijsttafel.* This starts off prosaically enough with soup plates and a dish of plain, steamed rice. The rice serves as a foundation for the contents of anywhere from 15 to 50 dishes, each more delectable than the one before. Some of these are described below. Sit down to this in the mood to stuff yourself, be prepared to feel as if you want to go to bed and sleep it off afterwards (which is what most Dutchmen do) and don't be surprised if you feel hungry again a few hours later. If moderation is your virtue, try the less ambitious *nasi goreng* or *bami goreng* (fried rice or noodles—with choice bits of meat, shrimp, chicken and the like). These are equally delicious and make fewer demands on your palate.

An average *rijsttafel* is usually enough for two people, although you would do well to add one or two extra dishes from among these: *Saté babi,* bite-sized morsels of pork skewered on a wooden spit and cooked in a mouth-watering *pinda* (peanut) sauce, is delicious. *Loempia* is a mixture of bean sprouts and vegetables wrapped in wafer-like pastry and fried in deep oil. *Kroepoek* is a large, crunchy prawn cracker. Fried prawns are a welcome addition. *Daging* is the general name for stewed meat. *Daging smoor* identifies the kind prepared in a black sauce and is particularly delectable. *Daging roedjak, daging besengek,* and *daging oppor* identify variations prepared in red, green and white sauces, respectively. *Bebottok* is meat steamed in coconut milk. *Fricadel* is a forced meat ball, relatively bland and somewhat mushy. *Sambal ati* is liver stewed in a red sauce. *Sambal telor* is an egg in red sauce. *Sambal oedang* are shrimps in a red sauce. *Babi pangang* is pieces of delicious roast suckling pig in a mild spicy sauce.

Ajam (chicken) is served in as many ways as meat. *Sambalans* is a collective term for several varieties of stewed vegetables, some of which you have probably never seen before.

Seroendeng, fried coconut and peanuts, is also called *apenhaar* (monkey hair). *Gado gado* are cold vegetables in peanut sauce. *Atjar ketimoen* are cucumber sticks in vinegar. *Pisang goreng* are fried bananas.

Roedjak is a compote of fresh fruit in a sweet sauce. *Sajor* means soup, and comes in a variety of guises, but is not a separate course as in most other countries.

To eat your *rijsttafel* you start off with a modest layer of rice on the bottom of your plate, adding a spoonful of each dish, arranging these neatly around the edge, finally filling in the center. It should be eaten with a spoon and fork. On a small dish you'll discover three or four little blobs of red and black paste—these are *sambals.* They are made of red peppers and spices and are generally red-hot. A little goes a long way. If you inadvertently bite into something that is painfully over-spiced the remedy is a large spoonful of plain rice.

Beer, though not Indonesian, is the perfect beverage to accompany a *rijsttafel.* Iced tea, lemonade or mineral water are also excellent. But never wine or milk.

Final Reminders

In nearly all Dutch restaurants, whether the cuisine be French, Indonesian or Serbo-Croatian, a service charge of 15 percent and a Value Added Tax (VAT) are included in the bill. This also applies to a *borrel* (a shot of Dutch gin) or any other drink in a bar or café. If you have any doubts, ask. Unless the service has been unusually atten-tive, you're at perfect liberty to pocket all your change, just as the average Dutchman does.

Remember, too, that the better Dutch restaurants are fairly formal. If you prefer casual dress at mealtime, pick a modest type of place or you'll feel awkward matching your sportswear against the headwaiter's white tie and tails. Dutch restaurants hardly ever have high chairs or children's portions, so the youngest members of your party will likely fare better at your hotel.

Because the Dutch follow the continental custom of relaxing at the table, allow at least an hour for a simple meal, two for something more elaborate. When short of time (or money) but brave enough to try a really cheap meal, try your hand at one of the "automatieks". A guilder or two in the slot and you pull out: a *croquetje*—a croquette with either veal or beef; a *loempia*—Chinese/Indonesian pancake roll; a *gehaktbal* —meat ball; a *nasibal*—Indonesian-version meat ball, rather hot, with rice; a *huzarensla*—Russian salad (cold hard-boiled egg with lettuce leaf, slice of tomato, gherkin).

If you intend to eat something at an automatiek, take care to have some guilders, as only some have change machines and it is not always possible to get your money changed.

All in all, eating is a delight in Holland, especially as nowadays there is no difficulty in finding places to suit every palate or fancy. True, it is expensive in most places, but the personal attention and service are often worth it. Moreover, a growing number of restaurants all over the country now serve the so-called tourist menu, which provides more than enough food for the average visitor (the Dutch themselves have tremendous appetites), and at a price about half the normal menu rates. So if you are traveling on a budget, look for the notices which announce "Tourist Menu."

THE DUTCH WAY OF LIFE

Dignity and Comfort

What the Dutch are today results mainly from two influences—water and religion. Both have stamped themselves on the Netherlands landscape, where they stare you in the face in the form of dikes and churches, and on the personality of the Netherlanders, though here these two influences may not always be so apparent.

To understand the Netherlander you have to know that about half of his compact little country has been wrested from the sea and that he stands over it in ceaseless vigil to prevent its reconquest, maintaining dams against the flood and running pumps to empty out the water infiltrating from below. That is the meaning of the quaint dikes and windmills that mark the Dutch countryside. He is holding his country aloft to keep it from slipping back into the sea. No one has given the

Dutchman anything; he has worked hard for what he has and must go on working to keep it.

The sense that life is no frolic is reinforced by their Calvinist beliefs; or perhaps Calvinism was attractive to such a people. Once Holland was a great Protestant fortress in Western Europe. Today the Roman Catholics, who a century ago were a small minority in the south, number about 40 percent of the population and, owing to a higher birth-rate, are increasing their numerical ratio. But it was a leading Catholic who said, "In Holland, the Catholics are Calvinistic, too!" Until recent years, Holland was a country of Sunday blue laws, although the Dutch are now operating more in harmony with modern liberality in these matters. Indeed in some cities, notably Amsterdam, any notion of censorship or puritanism has long since been abandoned with an unusual vigor. But there are still two or three rural villages where you are in danger of assault if you try to take photos on the Sabbath.

A grim fight for economic survival and a grim religion have made the Dutch basically serious, relatively humorless, hard-working, law-abiding, helpful, and hospitable. They have given them a sense of order, an inclination towards communal organization, a devotion to tradition and written precedents, and a passion for cleanliness and neatness, although in the late '60s and early '70s, the "absolute freedom" idea tended to turn Holland into a mecca for drop-outs creating a situation which the generally tolerant Dutch found hard to control effectively.

The water both unites and divides the land. The latticework of rivers and canals make every part of the Netherlands easily accessible; commerce and culture flowed freely through the country long before it was knitted together by railways and highways. Yet, paradoxically, the same water has created isolation, separating the north from the south, the islands from the mainland, one village from another. Because of this a day's drive will take you through many different collections of dialects and accents, customs and costumes. The dark, hard-bitten Protestant farmers of the island of Walcheren have little in common with the more jovial, Catholic farmers of Brabant just over the causeway. The people of Amsterdam have a different accent from those of Haarlem, a quarter-hour away by train.

The water has had other effects. The North Sea, gateway to the great currents of international trade, has brought to the west wealth, urbanity, denser population. The south and east are more agricultural, more insular, more tradition-bound. The Netherlands is many regions; the sea, the rivers, and the canals help to account for the differences.

It seems no mere coincidence that religious lines roughly follow water lines. One speaks of "above" or "below" the Moerdijk to denote the regions north and south of the great estuary, but also to signify the

Protestant and Catholic parts of the country, though the religious line has been growing more fuzzy in recent years.

Perhaps even more than the water, religion both unites and divides the Dutch. Nowhere else in Europe is there such a compartmentalization of society into denominational groups. Schools, hospitals, and similar benevolent organizations are administered by Roman Catholic or various Protestant confessions with state subsidies. A bare handful of newspapers are independent, the rest identifying themselves with Catholic, Protestant, or Socialist ideologies, as do radio and television organizations.

This factionalization penetrates every aspect of life. A Catholic house painter, for example, might typically be educated at a parochial school, join a Catholic sports club, meet a Catholic spouse at a denominational young people's dance, read a Catholic newspaper, subscribe to a Catholic weekly magazine, listen to the Catholic radio station, vote for the Catholic party candidates, trade at Catholic stores, spend his holidays on Catholic-sponsored excursions, have his appendix removed in a Catholic hospital, and end his days in a Catholic old peoples' home on a Catholic-managed old-age pension, all without ever knowing his Protestant neighbor, whose life might follow a similarly limited pattern. Indeed, Catholics distinguish themselves from Protestants by wearing their wedding ring on the third finger of their left instead of on the right. The distinction can be misleading, however, because a gold band often doubles as an engagement ring, in which case Protestants wear it on their *left* hands and Catholics on the *right.* Fortunately for the future of Holland, this pattern is beginning to change, especially in the larger urban centers to which the more ambitious and liberal youth of the countryside escape.

A Profile of the Dutch

In talking of the Dutch way of life, the aspects that the visitor does not immediately see have been purposely stressed. This background may help in an understanding of the Dutch personality, customs, and manners that will be discussed later.

With the big reservation that there is much diversity even in this little country, this is what the Dutch are like:

They are first and foremost home-loving people. The French and the Italians may make the café or bistro the center of their social life, but not the Dutch. They stay at home, in the bosom of the family—and an ample bosom it is, because the Dutch are still inclined to take literally the Biblical admonition to be fruitful and multiply. It is no wonder that the jam-packed people must plow the bottom of the sea in their frantic effort to avoid bursting out of their country.

The Dutch rise early and go to work mainly by car or public transport. Sandwiches used to be taken along too, but nowadays it is more usual to buy lunch in the canteen or one of the numerous snackbars. The end of the day is marked by an early dinner (6 P.M. is not considered too early). Then the evening is spent comfortably at home. They pore over the evening newspapers, which have been delivered. (Evening papers are more popular than morning editions because the Dutch do not believe in skimming through the headlines.) They may look at television, listen to the radio, play chess, practice a musical instrument, or they may just sit. This lifestyle, however, is changing with the under-35s, who prefer livelier diversions and know how to provide them.

Because home provides the center of life, a great deal of time and expense go into it, especially those parts that are open to public view. The living room must be ample and comfortable. More often than not it is over-furnished and over-endowed with knick-knacks. Particularly in cities, it will likely be the front room of a private house, its broad windows offering the nocturnal passerby an unobstructed view of family and guests, the most notable exception to the Dutch insistence on privacy. To draw the curtains would suggest that something illicit was intended . . . and would deprive the neighbors of the opportunity to admire and envy the new television set, the oil painting on the wall, the tableau of tourist gewgaws from holidays in Italy and Spain.

Competing with the home as a source of material satisfaction the automobile parked in front of the house now broadens the average Dutch family's leisure horizons. Although parking is difficult and distances are short enough to warrant greater use of public transport (especially in such a densely-populated country), the Dutchman makes greater use of the car than any other European. With one car to every four inhabitants—not counting at least half as many mopeds and bicycles as there are people—even the excellent network of motor highways, seen in 32.5 kilometers (20 miles) of roads per square kilometer compared with 17.8 in West Germany and 15.8 in Belgium, cannot carry peak time and holiday traffic without creating long queues. At busy weekends even the six-lane motorways often have three-mile files of waiting cars.

Almost every house has flowers—a cheerful garden, be it only a two-by-four plot, or pots and vases full of tastefully arranged blossoms. For here is where the Dutch may fool you. They may seem formidably stiff and unromantic, but the love of flowers is a national characteristic. In the spring they will travel for hours to see the tulip and hyacinth fields in bloom, and then return home laden with garlands and bouquets. Perhaps their love for flowers is a compensation for the drabness of their climate and the flatness of the land.

They will perplex you in other ways too. Without being very articulate about it, they are likely to enjoy music and to adore painting. It isn't for nothing that many provincial towns have their own symphony orchestra and almost every village at least one brass band and a choral society; it is no accident that museums are crowded, even in winter when the tourists are gone.

They are also a nation of sun-worshippers, which can easily be understood in a country where there is precious little sun to worship. They build big windows to let in whatever sunlight there is and, if Sunday happens to be bright, the whole family rush off to the beach or to the field to thrust their faces to the sun. Almost every Dutch person seems to be able to go to Italy, Spain or France for a holiday in the ceaseless quest for sunlight. More and more of them, too, now go winter-sporting to Austria or Switzerland to benefit from the mountain suns of January through March. A decade ago, the Dutch talked of sun with a kind of starved ardor. But today, they revel in being able to follow the sun on a grand scale.

Orderliness of Manners

If you visit Holland, you are likely, of course, to meet Dutchmen and women (though some resourceful British and American travelers have managed to avoid this, to a great extent, by staying at tourist hotels and then speeding through the countryside). They have their own manners and values, and it might be helpful to know something about them to avoid misunderstandings. It should be added, however, that you need not be too nervous about mistakes because the average Netherlander is supremely tolerant, not given to touchiness and has had sufficient contact with foreigners to make allowances for whatever mannerisms may not be understood. Hospitality towards foreigners and a willingness to make allowance for their transgressions are so great, particularly in western Holland, that some resident foreigners who have learned to speak Dutch make a practice of sticking to English to get the benefit of the preferential treatment reserved for strangers.

Social intercourse in the Netherlands is marked by fixed forms, literalness, and time-saving efficiency, and rests on the principle that everyone is a member of the same community. When a Dutch person walks into a train compartment, barbershop, or even washroom, they say "Good morning" or "Good afternoon" to all present and the rest are expected to reply. In a business or social gathering, he will introduce himself individually to everyone else, which is accomplished by a lightning handshake while barking out his surname. Unless the individual is accustomed to foreigners, he or she will be surprised by your greeting of "Hello!" or "How do you do?" Indeed, the latter form of greeting may bewilder her, and you might be stared at rather blankly, or treated to a description of how she *does* feel. The Dutch form of self-introduction is actually remarkably efficient and a boon to the harried hostess who does not remember the names of all her guests. If you, in the Anglo-American manner, enter a social gathering without introducing yourself personally to all the people who are present, they may be upset by your apparent casualness.

The Dutch are punctual in their appointments and expect you to be the same. If you are tardy, remember to make profuse apologies or they may feel slighted. Promptness in Holland is not a superficial thing; it springs from a sense of orderliness and from a feeling that it is an impermissible imposition to waste the time of others. There is a growing tendency to more casualness and less strict punctuality, but the Dutch are still more than likely to bring a bouquet of flowers, especially if it is the first visit to your home.

Because the Dutch tend to be literal, you must avoid saying any casual things that you do not exactly mean. If you say, "Drop in some time when you are in the neighborhood" as a rhetorical remark, they may, to your surprise, visit you. If you say, "I'll get in touch with you in a few weeks," they fully expect you to do it. They, on the other hand, mean precisely what they say and you can usually depend on it.

At first meetings, the Dutch are reserved to the point of seeming brusque. This is not because they are cold or hostile, but because they regard over-friendliness as an imposition on you. They have a strong sense of privacy, which is maintained in spite of the constant elbow-rubbing in this crowded country, and they will also respect your privacy. They will warm up considerably after subsequent meetings, if you encourage them to do so. However, do not expect vivacity. The flowery word with the light touch is not a Dutch characteristic. In sum, the Dutch, in their everyday contacts, are stiff, but dependable; reserved, but friendly; unimaginative, but intelligent and intellectually curious.

The Dutch way of life is ruled by rigid laws of etiquette, which you should try to understand, even if you do not observe them. A shop attendant will concentrate on one customer until she is ready to leave the shop, and will then see her to the door. This is vexing if you happen to be in a hurry, but it's no use trying to rush things. The other customer will look at you indignantly, and the attendant will get nervous.

Decorum and Coziness

Set forms of politeness run through every activity in which persons come in contact and, more than in most countries, formality is an accepted standard of all classes and groups. This is the country where breakfast will be served by a waiter in white tie and tails in a restaurant that you would consider second-class at home. *Dank u wel* (thank you) and *Als 't U blieft* (If you please) constantly interlard conversation. "Yes" and "no" are rarely spoken without being followed by "sir" or "madam." In Holland, these are not empty forms, but living courtesies among a people with tremendous respect for other human beings. There are set stereotypes for addressing letters. For example, a letter to you would probably be addressed *"Weledelgeboren Heer Smith"* (the "very nobly born Mr Smith"). Don't let it go to your head! If you were, say, a member of a baron's family, you would be addressed as "The highly well born . . ." Every rank in society has its form of address, though, increasingly, the more egalitarian forms *dhr* (Mr) and *mevrouw* (Ms or Mrs) are used.

The "Dutch treat" really exists. If you eat or drink with them, you are fully expected to pay your share—calculated down to the last cent—unless it has been decided in advance that you are a guest. You will be left in no doubt about the situation. If you are asked, "May I invite you?" or "Will you be my guest?" you know where you stand. A suggestion to "Join me for lunch" or "Let's have dinner together!" usually means Dutch treat. If a Dutchman does pay for you, normally you are expected to reciprocate at the first convenient opportunity. All of this does not apply if you, as a foreigner, are a guest in a Dutch home. Home hospitality to a visitor can have no counterpart, and none is expected. But you will cause delight if you take along a plant or bouquet, or send one the next day.

You can learn a great deal about a nation from its language. There are two commonly-used words in Dutch with so many connotations that they cannot be accurately translated. One is *deftig,* a concept that includes the qualities of dignity, respectability, decorum, and propriety. The other is *gezellig,* which embodies the ideas of coziness, comfort, and pleasure. Both are values highly cherished by the Dutch. You must see a septuagenarian granddame, managing to remain stately while astride a bicycle, to realize the *deftigheid* that is Holland. The word has, unfortuntely, fallen into disrepute among the young and has taken on the connotation of stuffiness and sham. But the yearning for respectability is dying hard.

For all their Calvinism, the Dutch love earthly pleasures, and the gold seal of approval for a comfortable living room, an animated party, a pleasant chat over beer or a *borrel* (a nip of Dutch gin) at a sidewalk café is the word *gezellig.* The Dutchman has fulfilled a primary aim in life if he or she manages to exude *deftigheid* while reveling in a *gezellig* evening. If these sound like bourgeois values, it is no wonder. The Dutch are essentially a bourgeois nation.

But the Dutch language also betrays the sentimentality beneath the *deftig* exterior in the profuse use of diminutives. In his doll's house of a country, it is not surprising that to make something small is also to invest it with affection. The Hollander's darling son Piet is called *Pietje*. And the beloved five o'clock nip of gin is a *borreltje.*

Another thing that betrays the sentimentality concealed behind a stolid exterior is the calendar of birthdays and other anniversaries, which often hangs in the bathroom. This may seem to you an odd place to hide such a calendar, but you must remember that the Dutchman does not wear his heart on his sleeve. Birthdays are really celebrated—usually by keeping open house from 10 in the morning until late at night. And woe betide the relative or friend who fails to put in an appearance bearing a bunch of flowers or a small present. Even small occasions, such as the anniversary of the office-boy or a secretary joining the office, have to be celebrated with cream cakes all round.

Until the late 1960s you would have had trouble comprehending the Dutchman's attitude towards women, which was simultaneously progressive and conservative, considerate and negligent. He had given his woman the vote, educated her more than women-folk in most countries, and dressed her well. But he would frequently ignore her in company, let her trail behind while walking down the street and would sometimes act as though he was not aware of her presence. But this has all changed now. Dutch women have been demanding full recognition in all spheres, including the home, and in most cases have been given it. Particularly has the younger generation been shouting for "freedom," and it is no unusual thing to see a laughing procession of young women, including wives, carrying banners which proclaim that "a woman is boss of her own body" and will "no longer be pushed around or ignored." They mean it, too. Even the teenage girls, who a few years ago were sternly kept in check by strict parents, now generally share with their mothers a liberated approach to life.

A Feeling for Organization

Dutch society is characterized by a high degree of organization. The density of the population makes this both necessary and possible. Almost everything the housewife needs is delivered to her door—not just milk and newspapers, but soap, meat, groceries, vegetables, fruit, bread. If she lives above the ground floor, she may have a pulley-operated basket with which she sends down her order and pulls up the supplies. This system of home delivery is possible because almost all Netherlanders live in closely settled areas. However, high wages, shortage of labor, and tall apartment buildings have combined to limit severely this personal service, a trend probably assisted by the competitive supermarkets and shopping centers springing up in residential areas.

The Dutch love to organize themselves, and they form societies for almost every conceivable purpose. On Sundays you will see hiking societies marching out, in serried ranks, for their self-regimented weekend pastime. There are religious, political, philanthropic, and social associations of every sort. Trade groups, chambers of commerce and research bodies multiply. Along with the associations go "plans." There are plans to drain what is left of the Zuider Zee, to industrialize marginal farm areas, to improve towns, and to raise the mortgage on the local tennis club.

The system of government is a constitutional monarchy, at whose pinnacle stands the throne, now occupied by Queen Beatrix, a modern, well-educated, and democratic woman who treats her function as a vocation rather than a divine right. She lives with her husband, Prince Claus, and her three sons in a palace situated in a wood on the outskirts of Den Haag (The Hague), called Huis ten Bosch. There is very little protocol. The children attend a progressive school and are shown no special favors. Queen Beatrix spent four years as an ordinary student at Leiden University. Of her sisters, Irene, recently divorced, has two sons and two daughters; Margriet, who also studied at Leiden University, married a commoner, Pieter van Vollenhoven, and has four sons; Christina, the youngest, married a Cuban exile working as a teacher in the States in 1975. They now have two children and are planning to set up house in the Netherlands. Although they are royal, this family epitomizes the middle-class virtues which have made the Dutch respected throughout the world, while at home, they have the sincere support of most of the Dutch people.

Dutch politics are ordinarily as placid as the people themselves and are seldom discussed, except in dramatic situations, such as occurred with the Lockheed scandal, in which Prince Bernhard, husband of the then Queen, Julianna, was involved, and the South Moluccan kidnappings, and hijackings of 1975 and 1977. In these situations, every Dutchman had an involved and morally thoughtout, if individual, opinion. This does not mean that the average citizen has no interest in the government. At the same time that he deplores bureaucratic waste and inefficiency, he may secretly envy his neighbor who has a safe job as a governmental civil servant or in the highly organized municipal administration that keeps track of his every change of address and every family detail. At the same time that he complains about endless red tape and stifling regulations, he may be urging a local ordinance to prevent unfair competition in his particular business by prohibiting competitors from keeping open after 6 P.M.

Domestic politics are dominated by problems typical of the '80s such as unemployment and the health of the economy. The uneasy coalition of Christian Democrats and conservative Liberals which governed from 1977 was replaced in 1981 by the resumed partnership of Christian Democrats and Socialists. However, the 1982 election showed an inclination towards the right, apparently from a desire to return to a more rigid control of the economy and, perhaps also as a result of the inherent conservatism of the people, exaggerated at this time of recession. Increasingly, there appears to be a tendency towards separating economic from religious issues. So intertwined are church and state, however, and so strong is the conviction that the moral approach to problems is the only correct one that this movement continues to be slow.

The Dutch Economy

The Dutch are traditionally a trading nation and only adopted full-scale industrialization after World War II. For many years, reconstruction and rapid industrialization kept employment and production at consistently high levels. The average Dutch wage increased nearly four-fold, with a consequent increase in the standard of living. Less than 6% of the working population is now involved with the traditional occupations of fishing and agriculture. (in 1930 these sectors accounted for over 20%). There has over recent years also been a tendency for Dutch industry to become capital intensive instead of labour intensive as a result of rising labor costs. This has resulted in relatively high levels of unemployment and is one of a number of serious social problems still to be resolved.

The Dutch economy benefited greatly from the creation of the European Economic Community (EEC). Over 70% of Holland's exports now go to its EEC partners and some 30% of all goods entering the EEC from overseas countries now pass through Dutch ports. Rotterdam has become, literally, the trading gateway to Europe.

Over the last few years, however, there have been signs that Holland's economy is deteriorating. Higher energy prices and the change in the international economic order have unfortunately coincided with the depletion of Holland's only natural resource—gas, the revenue from which had sustained Dutch wages and social services at a very high level. Holland's economic problems are not unique, but the natural thriftiness of the Dutch and the highly controlled nature of their society have helped to maintain its currency at a high level of convertability. These same qualities may also mean that the country could well benefit more quickly from the world's hoped-for emergence from the current economic recession.

ENGLISH-DUTCH VOCABULARY

USEFUL EXPRESSIONS

English	Dutch
Please	Alstublieft
Thank you very much	Dank U zeer
Good morning, sir	Dag, Mijnheer
Good evening, madam	Goedenavond, Mevrouw
Good night	Goede nacht
Goodbye	Tot ziens
Excuse me	Neem me niet kwalijk
I understand, I don't understand	Dat begrijp ik, dat begrijp ik niet
Hunger, thirst	Honger, dorst
I am hungry, thirsty	Ik heb honger, dorst
Yes, no	Ja, nee
Yesterday, today, tomorrow	Gisteren, vandaag, morgen
This evening, this morning	Vanavond, vanmorgen
How much?	Hoeveel?
Expensive, cheap	Duur, goedkoop
Where? Where is? Where are?	Waar? Waar is? Waar zijn?
Is this the right way to . . . ?	Is dit de goede weg naar . . . ?
Can you direct me to the nearest . . . ?	Kunt u mij . . . diehtsbijzijnde . . . bijzijnde . . . wijzen?
doctor	de . . . dokter
hotel/restaurant	het . . . hotel/restaurant
garage	de . . . garage
post office	het . . . postkantoor
police station	het . . . politiebureau
telephone	de . . . telefoon
Left, right	Links, rechts
To the left/right	Naar links/rechts
Bus/trolley stop	Bus/tram halte
Church	Kerk
Theater	Theater
Movie theater (cinema)	Bioscoop
Entrance	Ingang
Exit	Uitgang
Admission free	Vrije toegang
Open from . . . to . . .	Geopend van . . . tot . . .

No smoking	Verboden te roken
Gentlemen	Heren
Ladies	Dames
Town Hall	Stadhuis
Art Gallery	Schilderijenmuseum
Cathedral	Kathedraal (domkerk)

RESTAURANTS AND DINING

Please give us the menu	Kag ik het menu zien?
What do you recommend?	Wat kunt U aanbevelen?
Please give us the table d'hôte	Wij nemen table d'hôte
Please serve us as quickly as possible	Bedien ons zo vlug mogelijk, alstublieft
Please give me the check (bill)	Ober, kan ik betalen?
Have you included the tip?	Is dit inclusief?
Waiter! Waitress!	Ober! Juffrouw!
Please give us some . . .	Geeft u ons wat . . .
Bread and butter	Boterham
Toast	Geroostered brood
buttered	warm gesmeerd
dry	zonder boter
Jam	Jam
Marmalade	Marmelade
Cheese	Kaas

Eggs

Bacon and eggs	Eieren met spek
Fried eggs	Spiegeleieren
Boiled egg	Gekookt ei
soft-boiled	zachgekookt
medium	halfzacht
hard-boiled	hardgekookt
scrambled	roerei

Fish

Cod	Kabeljauw
Flounder	Bot
Eel	Paling
Halibut	Heilbot
Herring	Haring
Mackerel	Makreel
Plaice	Schol
Salmon	Zalm

Trout	Forel
Crab	Krab
Crayfish	Rivierkreeft
Lobster	Kreeft
Oysters	Oesters
Shrimp	Garnalen

Meat

Spring chicken	Piepkuiken
Chicken	Kip
Duck	Eend
Wild duck	Wilde eend
Goose	Gans
Partridge	Patrijs
Rabbit	Konijn
Hare	Haas

Pork Chops	Varkenskotelet
Roast lamb	Gebraden lamsvlees
Roast mutton	Gebraden schapenvlees
Roast veal	Gebraden kalfsvlees
Roast beef	Rosbief

Fried	Gebakken
Roasted	Gebraden
Smoked	Gerookt
Stewed	Gestoofd
Rare	Bleu, rrod
Medium	Half gaar
Well done	Goed gaar

Vegetables

Asparagus	Asperges
Beans	Bonen
String beans	Snijbonen
Green beans (French beans)	Sperciebonen
Brussels sprouts	Brusselse spruitjes
Cabbage	Kool
Carrots	Worteltjes
Cauliflower	Bloemkool
Cucumber	Komkommer
Mushrooms	Champignons
Onions	Uien
Peas	Doperwten

Potatoes	Aardappelen
boiled	gekookte
fried	gebakken
French-fried	Pommes frites
mashed	Aardappelpuree
Rice	Rijst
Sauerkraut	Zuurkool
Spinach	Spinazie
Tomatoes	Tomaten
Turnips	Koolraap
Lettuce, salad	Sla

Fruit

Apple	Appel
Cherries	Kersen
Grapes	Druiven
Lemon	Citroen
Orange	Sinaasappel
Pears	Peren
Fruit salad	Vruchtensla

Drinks

A bottle of . . .	Een fles . . .
A pot of . . .	Een potje . . .
A glass of . . .	Een glas . . .
A cup of . . .	Een kop . . .

Water	Water
Iced water	IJswater
Mineral water	Mineraalwater
Milk	Kelk
Coffee	Koffie
Coffee with hot milk/cream	Koffie met hete melk/room
Tea, iced tea	Thee, thé glacé
Hot chocolate	Warme chocolade
Beer	Bier

Wine (red, white)	Wijn (rode, witte)
Sugar	Suiker
Salt	Zout
Pepper	Peper
Mustard	Mosterd

AT THE HOTEL

Can you recommend a good hotel?	Kunt u me een goed hotel aanbevelen?
Which is the best hotel?	Wat is het best hotel?
Have you anything cheaper?	Hebt u iets goedkoper?
What is the price including breakfast?	Wat is de prijs met ontbijt?
Does the price include service?	Geldt de prijs inclusief bediening?
At what time is . . .	Hoe laat is . . .
breakfast	het ontbijt
lunch	het middageten
dinner	het avondeten
Please wake me at . . . o'clock	Ik wil graag om . . . uur gewekt worden
I want this dry-cleaned	Kunt U dit laten stomen?
I want these clothes washed	Wilt U alstublieft deze kleren in de was doen
I would like to have a . . .	Ik zou . . . willen hebben
single room	een eenpersoonskamer
double room with	een kamer met
twin beds	twee bedden
double bed	een tweepersoonsbed
with bath	met bad
Another pillow	Nog een kussen
Another blanket	Nog een deken
Soap, towel	Zeep, handdoek
Coat-hangers	Klerenhangers

TRAVELING BY TRAIN

Timetable	Dienstregeling
Through train	Doorgaande trein
Slow train	Stoptrein
Fast train	Sneltrein
Express train	Exprestrein
Weekdays only	Alleen werkdagen
Sundays and holidays only	Alleen zon- en feestdagen
Return ticket	Retour
One-way ticket	Enkele reis
Fare	Prijs van het biljet
Compartment	Coupé
Dining car	Restauratiewagen
Sleeping compartment	Slaapcoupé
First class	Eerste class
Second class	Tweede klas
Delay	Aansluiting

Connection	Vertraging
All aboard	Instappen

AT THE POST OFFICE

Air mail	Luchtpost
Ordinary mail	Gewone post
Special delivery	Expresse
Cable	Telegram
Stamp	Postzegel
Registered	Aangetekend
Insured	Verzekerd

MOTORING

How many kilometers is it to . . . ?	Hoeveel kilometers is het naar . . . ?
I want . . . liters of gasoline	Ik wens . . . liter benzine
Fill it up, please	Bijvullen, alstublieft
Will you . . .	Wilt U . . .
grease the car	de wagen doorsmeren
change the oil	de olie vernieuwen
check the oil	de olie controleren
wash the car	de wagen wassen
clean the windscreen (windshield)	de voorruit schoonmaken
top up the battery with distilled water	de accu met gedistilleerd water bijvullen
change this wheel	dit wiel verwisselen
test the tyre (tire) pressures	de spanning van de banden controleren
fill the radiator	de radiateur bijvullen
There is something wrong with . . .	Er mankeert iets aan . . .
I will come for the car at . . . o'clock	Ik zal de wagen om . . . uur komen halen
What will it cost?	Hoeveel kost dat?
May I park here?	Mag ik hier parkeren?
Axle (back)	Achteras
Axle (front)	Vooras
Bearing	Lager
Body	Carrosserie
Bonnet (hood)	Kap
Brake	Rem
Carburetor	Carburator
Clutch	Koppeling
Crankshaft	Krukas
Cylinder	Cylinder
Dashboard	Instrumentenbord

Exhaust	Uitlaat
Bumper	Bumper
Gear box	Versnellingsbak
Headlights	Koplampen
Ignition	Ontsteking
Jet or carburetor	Sproeier
Number plate	Nummerplaat
Oil can	Oliekan
Petrol tin (gas can)	Benzineblik
Spark(ing) plug	Bougie
Speedometer	Snelheidsmeter
Steering wheel	Banden
Tyres (tires)	Stuurwiel
Tail light	Achterlicht
Valve	Klep (van de motor)
Wheel (spare)	Wiel (reserve)
Windscreen wiper	Ruitenwisser
The toolbox	Gereedschapskist
Bolt	Bout
File	Vijl
Hammer	Hamer
Jack	Crick
Nail	Spijker
Nut	Moer
Pliers	Buigtang
Screw	Schroef
Sound your horn	Klaxoneren, signaal geven
Slow	Langzaam
Proceed at walking pace	Stapvoets rijden
To the right	Naar rechts
To the left	Naar links
Crossroads	Kruispunt
No admission	Verboden toegang/inrit
Keep to your right	Rechts houden
Level crossing	Spoorwegkruising
Road up for repair	Opgebroken rijweg
Road blocked	Versperde weg
No traffic allowed	Verboden voor alle verkeer
One-way street	Eenrichtingverkeer
Traffic lights	Verkeerslichten
Turn	Keren
Straight ahead	Rechtuit of Rechtdoor
Maximum speed	Maximum snelheid

(Vocabulary continued on page 104)

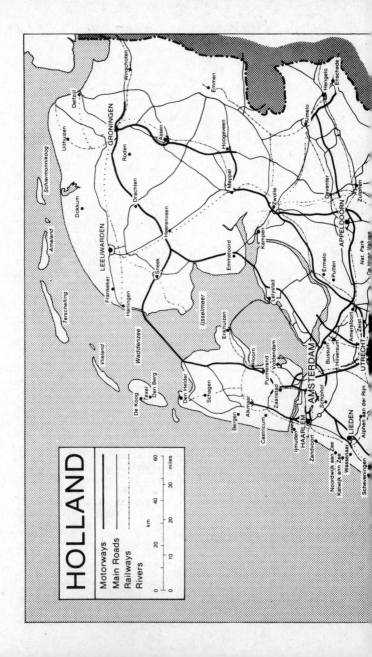

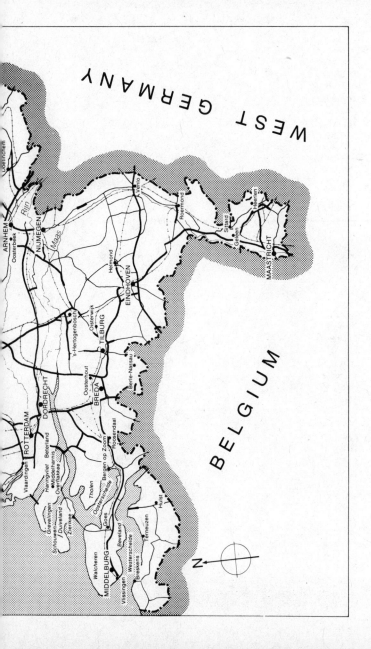

DAYS OF THE WEEK

Monday	maandag
Tuesday	dinsdag
Wednesday	woensdag
Thursday	donderdag
Friday	vrijdag
Saturday	zaterdag
Sunday	zondag

NUMERALS

one	een (ayn)
two	twee (tvay)
three	drie (dree)
four	vier (feer)
five	vijf (fife)
six	zes (sess)
seven	zeven (zayfern)
eight	acht (ahgt)
nine	negen (nayghen)
ten	tien (teen)
eleven	elf (elf)
twelve	twaalf (tvahlf)
thirteen	dertien (derrteen)
fourteen	veertien (fairteen)
fifteen	vijftien (fifeteen)
sixteen	zestien (zessteen)
seventeen	zeventien (zayfenteen)
eighteen	achttien (ahgteen)
nineteen	negentien (nayhgenteen)
twenty	twintig (tvintuhk)
twenty-one	een en twintig (ayn en tvintuhk)
twenty-two	twee en twintig (tvay en tvintuhk)
thirty	dertig (derrtuhk)
forty	veeertig (fairtuhk)
fifty	viftig (fifetuhk)
sixty	zestig (zesstuhk)
seventy	zeventig (zayfentuhk)
eighty	tachtig (tahktuhk)
ninety	negentig (naygentuhk)
one hundred	honderd (hondert)
one hundred and ten	honderd tien (hondert teen)
two hundred	tweehonderd (tvay hondert)
one thousand	duizend (doyzent)